The Pains and Pleasures of Parenthood

Lib Uzzell Griffin

BEDLAM PRESS
52 Glenmore-Dunbarton
Durham, NC 27707

ISBN: 0-9636705-0-6

Dewey Decimal Classification: 649
Subject Heading: PARENTING
Library of Congress Catalog Number: 84-23911
Printed in the United States of America

Library of Congress Cataloging in Publication Data

Griffin, Lib Uzzell, 1917-
The pains and pleasures of parenthood.

1. Parenting—United States—Anecdotes, facetiae, satire, etc. 2. Parenting—Religious aspects—Christianity. I. Title.
HQ755.8.G745 1993 649'1 84-23911
ISBN: 0-9636705-0-6

Produced by JM Productions, Brentwood, TN 37024-1911

To all my children and grandchildren;
they are the sunshine of my life.
To Chief, who made me what I am—
a mother!

Contents

Introduction

I like surprises and have been blessed with nine of them.

I am a woman of four religions. I was born an Episcopalian, married a Methodist who went to a Baptist school and practiced Catholicism.

I have the missionary zeal. I caught it from my Mom's cousin, a missionary to China, who was dedicated to saving the girl babies from the brink. I love all babies; I save old clothes; I try to teach my heathen. I like to live dangerously.

I believe life is a heavenly gift. I love the one He gave me. I almost didn't receive it. Premature, they wrapped me in cotton like a cocoon. It took me awhile to become the fat, free, butterfly that I am—still enjoying His gift.

I believe God has a plan for us. I went from the incubator to a big hotel oven. I've been in one ever since.

I believe life is to be celebrated. My full household sounds like a celebration. Full of noise. Full of mischief. Full of love.

I really love that "abundant life." Our Heavenly Father sent His Son to teach us to live a more abundant life. If mine were any more abundant, I'd bust.

"Ask and you shall receive." I have been asking and receiving. Asking and receiving. That's what this book is all about. My cup runneth over!

1
The Groom Was a Drip
(or Wedding Weepers)

Next to baptism and the Lord's Supper, I consider the solemnization of matrimony the most thought-provoking church service.

Solemn is right. My wedding was such a solemn occasion the groom cried all the way through it. I didn't. I have this abominable trait of enjoying everything. There's no time for tears. Enjoy. Enjoy.

After all, I was tired of running away from all those broken hearts I left behind. The chase was over. I felt relief in the air—my mother's. I had survived seven years of courtship. Friends would hear my new problems—really new and probably really little, like babies. The groom had already named six children. Between breakups and makeups. I was to be the lucky mother, the chosen one, today's bride.

I had been a reluctant schoolteacher, average artist, embryonic actress, enthusiastic dancer, but never a bride. Matrimony was to be a much later chapter, like at age thirty. I had other plans. Somehow all my plans were sprinkled with men. They were to help me get a job, change my flat tires or introduce me to another great guy. I could not live without them all and did not want to live with any one of them. That is until "Chief" came along.

Chief, like heap big Injun, came galloping into my life, upsetting all my well-laid plans. He still does. You can't get tired of him. He gallops in and gallops out, always carrying his bow and arrows. He squinted at the braves who helped my days and brightened my nights. He was Chief then. He is Chief now. Not just now and then.

As this maiden floated down the aisle on her wedding day, behind the sea of bridesmaids, I anxiously looked for Chief, my groom. He was the one floating on a sea of tears. Heavens, so was his best man, his brother. Wedding Weepers! My eyes anchored on the wedding party. Three preachers stood before me. Three buoys. Two of them were my uncles. Chief's idea. There was no powwow. When he ties a knot, it is tied.

My ninety-year-old great-uncle gave the "dearly beloved" bit without a tremor of voice or hand. He was already in tune with celestial things.

My fifty-year-old uncle gave the "I require and charge ye both, as ye will answer at the dreadful day of judgment when the secrets of all hearts shall be disclosed. . . ." (Those tears! Must be some secret!) . . ."that if either of you know any impediment. . . ." (We put up a good fight against the curse of love. We can't live without each other.)

My thirty-year-old minister gave "those whom God hath joined together, let no man put asunder." It should read—"let no man, woman, child, or sport put asunder."

The two optional prayers of the service deserve special attention. One asked for "the gift and heritage of children." I found out you'd better be careful what you pray for, or you just might get it.

The other prayer was for the home—"that their home may be a blessing and of peace." Ours has more mess and more bless than I thought possible. Certainly more pieces than peace, but no person with a soul attuned to spiritual things can hear the marriage vows and easily forget them. I have nine reminders.

2
The Bride Was a Deluge
(or The Unblenching Butterfly)

They say—Love is a merry-go-round and marriage keeps it on the square! How square can you get? I thought the pill was a person to be avoided. I thought the best contraceptive was *no*!

On dates I was often an onion eater or bubble gum popper. Sometimes I was full of information. Quick to tell male operators they had the wrong number—me—if their intentions were dishonorable. If an unexpected move caught me off guard, I have even resorted to "Have you been saved?"

Sometimes swains got the busy signal. Always I thanked them for calling. I did like the phone to ring.

As a single, I loved to mingle, mingle. Crowds were my thing. I shared my understanding, my laughs, my attention. I guarded my reputation, my self-respect, my bargaining power, and my body—my most precious possession, my gift from God.

Was I born too soon? Should I have shopped around like many do today? Chief got all of me. I was married at twenty-three; had my first child at twenty-five. Nine children, one at the time. Just think how many I could have had!

When I married Chief, I lost a dear friend but gained a lover. I have never been disappointed. Momentarily dismayed, dissatisfied, or disgusted—but never disappointed. At times he was friend, lover, friend-lover. Good friends never disappoint you. As they say, a friend can watch you make a fool of yourself and know you're not doing a permanent job. I have been blessed with lots of friends—but only one lover, Chief. Not that I don't have a sense of adventure. My marriage is like that. An adventure.

I understand men have appetites, habits, and traits that are as predictable as sunrise. How did I end up with a moonlight gambler? Philippians 4:19 reminds us that "God will supply all that you need from His glorious resources. . . ." That also includes the people with whom you need to live. I must need plenty.

Plenty of mutual likes and dislikes surfaced during my seven-year friendship with Chief. We both like people, activity, and homemade ice cream. We both dislike extreme heights, lightning, and complainers.

A two-year courtship was full of promises. As they say, he took me out, took me in, and took me for granted. He promised my mom he'd take care of me. Man, has he taken care of me!

He promised to be generous. He has always given me more than I asked for. If I needed a loaf of bread, he'd bring four. I'd switch my menu to sandwiches. If I needed a smidgin of okra for soup, he'd haul in a peck. There's enough okra in the deepfreeze for ten years. We wanted at least six children. He provided nine—more to love.

Marriage has agreed with me. It has *broadened* me. It has provided loads of laughs and moments of mystery. Can you give me a clue why Chief, a dentist, can fill a colorless cavity but can't close a dresser drawer? Why as an avid golfer, he knows which club to use to reach the green, but can't handle burned-out lights? Why he has a smashing forehand in tennis but can't dial a telephone?

Marriage has agreed with him. It has broadened him too. It has provided him with a built-in straight man for his jokes and buck-passing receptacle—me. He has made a few discoveries. I don't cook, act, or look like his mother. If it can be broken, soiled, or burnt, I will. I am slow until he drops the word "go." He found out it was my middle name. Not all nests belong to birds. There's a nest of books by my bed.

I am full of buttons. He knows which ones to push. Sometimes mine will get stuck, like the "I-love-you.-I love-you-I-love-you-" button. Once I pushed a few of his. Honesty answered the age-old question, "Why don't you ever tell me you love me?" "I told you once" was the reply. Puzzled, I pushed Explain and Clarify in rapid succession.

"Now let's get one thing straight," boomed the answer, "I told you once! I'm not going through our married life whimpering, 'I love you.' I never told another girl, 'I love you.' I go to work every day. I come home every night. I give you all my worldly goods. What more do you want? My life's blood? I don't intend to go around saying, 'I love you.' I intend to *show* you."

He has shown me and shown me. My old writing professor used to say about that overworked word "sex"—"Those who write about it, read about it, talk about it—they ain't got it!" As The Good Book says:

> That is how husbands should treat their wives, loving them as parts of themselves. For since a man and his wife are now one, a man is really doing himself a favor and loving himself when he loves his wife (Eph. 5:28, TLB).

3
Heavenly Hosts
(or One Little Thing After Another)

Things can get mighty complicated. Christmas, for instance, used to be so simple when your own mom took care of it. Newlyweds know the honeymoon is over when their first Christmas or birthday comes around. "We did it this way in my family," goes the cry. It doesn't get easier.

The first thing I did to complicate Christmas was get married. I can't believe I chose December twenty-eighth for my wedding day. I really fouled up my family's Christmas. Sweet and understanding, they had no complaints. Young and in love, I didn't know what day it was. I admit I received the most exciting Christmas present ever—a good husband —Chief.

War years prompted couples to take the big jump. Nothing was promised, only the here and now. That was enough. I thought it was great. There were no silver wedding gifts. Metals were used for bullets. There was nothing to polish.

All was not dull that first Christmas away from our homes. There was no tinsel for our first Christmas tree. No ornaments. No lights. Only Christmas cards and ribbons for decorations.

We were 800 miles from home, thanks to Uncle Sam. Chief had duty at the Air Corps base. I wasn't lonesome. I had our first baby, a two-month old girl blessing, to keep me company. I read the Christmas story from our Bible. There were carols on the radio. There was joy from the presence of our Heavenly Father. He had made another special day.

Complicated Christmases or birthdays vanish through the years. Soon, loving couples think as one. Certainly Christmases and birthdays are lovingly entwined in my mind. No sacrilege intended. As I look at my own babies, the power of God's love is understood. The miracle of miracles. Unbelievable. Unconditional love. Undeserved. Babies. Tremendous gifts. Life!

That Christmas, I recalled my first child's birth. I remember my fleeting doomsday thoughts. *So far away from home. A strange town. A strange doctor. A strange condition.* The feelings of finality, as they led me to the labor room. Feelings of abandonment as the door closed on Chief's helpless look. Feelings of reality. This job I do alone. No Chief. No Mama.

Then came the Heavenly Nudge: "I am with you always" (see Matt. 28:20). I picked up my protective armor. "Be strong and of good courage; be not afraid, neither be thou dismayed; for the Lord thy God is with thee whithersoever thou goest" (see Josh. 1:9). Even strapped to a cold hospital table, you feel that Blessed Assurance—warm and loved.

How comforted I felt repeating the Twenty-Third Psalm. As I whispered, "I will dwell in the house of the Lord forever," strange things began to happen. Maybe it was the anesthesia that sent my mind whirling down a human well. First I felt my own mother's arms. I was gently lifted from my mom to her mom, to her mom. On and on. Faster and faster I was passed from one set of arms to another, quietly and swiftly to Mary's arms—the mother of Jesus! As she cradled me in her arms, she smiled that smile God gives mothers. Such brilliance. Such understanding. Such beauty. Such joy!

I had been plied with pills, punched with needles and muffled with gas. I was sometimes with it, sometimes out of it. But my moment with Mary was eternal, special, mine.

4
Other Little Things
(or Doing What Comes Naturally)

No matter how you feel about numbers, they are always with us. If not, you get a call from the Internal Revenue Service. Numbers just don't interest me. I can tell you if something is blue-green or yellow-green. I can't tell you how far it is to the next town. I admit it. I carried my first child ten months, and the wags said I couldn't count. So the next time I was pregnant, the medics counted for me. I carried all nine of mine ten months. It was my cycle. My mom carried hers eight. It simply takes time to turn out a super product, and I had super babies. Thanks be to God!

My children loved numbers. "How many days to Christmas?" My husband, too: "How many more minutes before you're ready?" Friends also get in on it. "How much bacon does it take for your breakfast?" Believe me, when you're plowing through that mountain of bacon, you aren't counting. You're frying.

Chief is interested in numbers for another reason. When our babies meandered in early January instead of the expected December due date, he was shaken up. Another hoped-for tax deduction down the drain.

Each of my children has a number. I really *can* remember their names—on good days, my thinking days. They declare it is easier to say, "I'm number 4, 6, or 9" than "I'm Ted, Jeter, or Steve." They're just with it. My offspring and our government both insist we are numbers. Funny. They don't like to be called problems but don't mind being called numbers.

Chief calls them his investments. He declares he'd be a millionaire if all his investments paid off like that: "Lib and I always get more than expected." My financial jargon is, "I can't add or subtract, but I certainly can multiply." No one disagrees. I rarely use one of my favorites, "Marriage is an investment. If you show a little interest, it will pay dividends." I'm already in enough trouble.

Our children not only prefer to sign things with their number, but they mark their socks and emblazon their T-shirts. I just wish they wouldn't insist on introducing themselves by their numbers.

My child #2—#1 son—will have it no other way. He likes his number better than his nicknames. "Tyke, Buddy, and Butch" bring glares. Just don't call him "Junior"! After all, what can you expect of child #2—#1 son—whose mother stuffed herself with three pounds of grapes on his birthday? His due date was in December. January came. As I waited, I had time to conjure up cravings. It was malaga grapes for me. The morning of #2 child's birth, I inhaled an extra pound hidden from Christmas. That afternoon an observant neighbor brought me another pound. The third pound was a peace offering from Chief. He had spent the day golfing. He respects cravings.

My ten-month anxiety had nothing to do with taking my own razor to the hospital. The dull-razor prep before #1 was unforgettable. I was forewarned. There would be no nuns at this hospital like at my first birthing. This was a military facility—no water or bedpans except on regular rounds. What can you expect for a dollar a day? Certainly no complaints.

Thirteen months before, I had had a leisurely two weeks

in bed after childbirth. Now the new plan was to see whose patients could be pushed out of bed first. My strong knees but weak nerves were soothed by a fellow Carolinian who helped with the delivery. He dubbed our son, "Tarheel." I felt relieved he didn't call him, "Grapehead."

Three out of nine children chose January to come bless us. Child #3—#2 son—was born in a snowstorm, a rarity in Piedmont Carolina. Chief celebrated by making snow cream for the two knee babies before trudging through the white stuff to view his third offspring at the hospital. Most husbands didn't make it. Chief was the star attraction of the maternity ward—knocking snow off his boots, warming everyone with his smile. I felt special.

Sometimes it isn't easy to announce the coming of a new offspring, especially to your mother-in-law. After our second child was born, she said, "Isn't that nice? You have your family. One of each kind." Chief admitted he never divulged our family game plan to his mom. That quickly became "his job." He bravely prepared her for the little ones hopefully to come. After all, chiefs are supposed to be brave.

It was easier to tell the older children that another blessing was on the way. They loved babies. I remember how delighted Child #2—#1 son—was when I told him his ninth birthday present was a baby brother. Well, almost. This slowpoke, Child #6—#5 son—came a day past the birthday. His tardiness was forgiven when Child #2 saw him. He exclaimed, "Gee, Mom, this is the cutest one yet!" We shared a laugh as we admired the newborn, remembering we had said that about each one.

Most babies have the decency to come in the early morning. You can slip into the hospital while the other children are in bed. Of course, some have to be different. Instead of choosing some unearthly hour, child #4—#3 son—came at a very Godly hour: 11:00 AM Sunday. His was the easiest birth of all. It didn't seem like smooth sailing at first. Chief had taken the older two children to Sunday School. He left child #3—#2 son—with me. This usually unflappable toddler excitedly shook his finger at me when signs of impending birth appeared. He followed me, reprimanding, "Mommy, pot pot. Mommy, pot pot!" I was trying to get hospital transportation. Chief's father became so excited when I called him, he cut himself shaving. He sent a daughter.

When we reached the hospital, they declared there was no room. They called another hospital. Still no room. Shades of Mary, Jesus' mother! I told them I didn't want a room. I wanted a table. Not an examining table, a delivery table. The dear Lord was with me again. He sent me child #4—#3 son—so fast, there was only time for joy. So blessed. Having babies was no worse than having a bad cold. Thanks be to God. Not that anyone's seen a good cold. They're just a little inconvenient.

It was mighty inconvenient having a July baby, especially in a record-breaking heat wave. Child #5—#4 son—put in his appearance—the only summertime baby in the batch. Chief didn't seem to mind going out late at night for ham biscuits. Couldn't sleep anyway from the heat. True to form, this child is a ham lover and a nut fiend. What can you expect with a mother nutty enough to have a baby in July? The other eight children declare him—"The best one." Could it be because he is quiet, not a ham like his mom?

After five boys we had a welcomed change, another girl. Child #7—#2 girl—was a great Christmas present, even if she did arrive December 26. Chief, who faintly resembles Santa Claus, was understandably tired that Christmas day. He had the whole load. Heavy with child, I wasn't the swiftest, most helpful critter around. When Santa finished his visit, he was ready to hit the sack. No sack for me. Number

7 was on the way. Armed with a red nightgown, in honor of the season, Chief marched me to the hospital. Again I was filled with joy, exuberant for a legitimate excuse to leave the after-Christmas debris.

I was the only maternity case that night. The nursing authorities seized this opportunity to let their student nurses watch a live birth. My bed was lined with curious females, who were *all eyes.*

The supervisor was an enthusiastic informer. She quickly pointed out any significant changes in my welfare. Everyone had a turn seeing for themselves. I thought about selling tickets. What a performance! A mother of six about to have number seven. That I could do, thanks to the good Lord.

The nurses seemed disappointed in my performance. One whispered, "She can't be in labor. She hasn't yelled yet!" They couldn't fathom why I was so happy. Even when I was rolled into the delivery room, they eyed me suspiciously. They hadn't experienced the joy of unloading a bundle from heaven. They hadn't learned about God's timing. He has it all figured out perfectly. By the time you carry a baby nine months, you don't think about impending pain or discomfort. Let's just get it over with. You don't even care what it is. The nurses asked the inevitable question, "Do you want a girl or a boy?" I gave them my standard answer. "I don't care if it's a boy or girl, just so it's one or the other."

Chief and I built a new house. We named our wigwam, "Bedlam." All it needed to make it a home was a baby. Child #8—#6 son—made this unique contribution. He was so unique, he came into this world feet first. No amount of persuasion could turn him around. He has the prettiest head of all. I thank the precious Lord for that, because all my ease of birthing came to a screeching halt. I found myself in an impossible situation. My own doctor was operating elsewhere. I was in labor with an intern taking care of me. He was from South America. "South America, Take It Away." They don't speak our language too well and vice versa. And they don't regard childbirth the same way. His long, pointed fingernails made his examinations tortuous. A veteran of seven births, I calmly declared myself ready for the delivery room. My words fell on deaf ears. Nurses were making their holiday plans. It was early December. I repeated my plea. Fingernails were felt, black eyes flashed. His head shaking, "No! No!" Every "Yes! Yes!" of mine went unnoticed.

What to do? If the baby was positioned head first, I'd drop it. Feet first might be a little risky. I asked my Heavenly Father one more time, "What are *we* going to do?" Silence. Then He sent me an internationally known word, *sue!* Next time "black eyes" came near, I motioned him closer. When he leaned down, I whispered, "If I get out of this alive and anything happens to this baby, I'm gonna' *sue* the daylights out of you!" That brought action. In record time, child #8—#6 son—was delivered. In beautiful shape. More thanksgiving. More joy. Would you believe he has always loved South American food, especially chili? That he has a wife named "Sue" with big black eyes?

Eight wasn't enough. Child #8—#6 son—needed someone to play with. My idea. I bargained for six children. After six, what difference does one more make? Love has no limitations. There is always room in my heart for one more.

The youngest of our tribe, child #9—#7 son—declares he's the icing on the cake. He's convinced me. All sweetness and joy. Chief named him en route to the hospital. I didn't have a boy's name picked. The law of averages were in favor of a girl. We always chose a name from each side of our family. I was out of boy's names. Chief named him Stephen for the first Christian martyr. Chief declared we needed all the help we could get. As usual he is so right.

When this last child was born, I was back in my room

after giving birth. The morning shift of nurses was receiving orders. My doctor had gone to keep his office hours. Chief called a friend who lived nearby to come "look in on me." A Heavenly Nudge prompted her to run over immediately. An ex-nurse at the hospital, she could visit anytime. One look at my face and she flung back the covers. I was lying in a pool of blood. Pronto, she found help. So did I. Once again my Heavenly Father was looking after me. He knows our every need before we do. Even with every breath, how can we thank Him enough?

5
The Numbers Racket
(or Welcome to Bedlam)

A large family. How is it? Simple math. Everything is multiplied, and that suits me. The joys. The sorrows. The fun. The work. I don't want anything added, don't want anything subtracted. It's a constant source of wonder. You wonder if you can survive. You wonder if the house can survive.

There was no problem with our first nest, built with love, dreams, and prayers, and furnished with family rejects. There is no decor comparable to military make-do. It definitely spawned "eclectic." Inside, our quarters looked fairly normal. Outside, a backyard of live chickens was circumspect. No Southerner I know of can live without chicken.

Chief, a dentist, was attached to the station hospital. We ate well. Butchers have teeth, too. Whether in the commissary or dental chair, there was mutual courtesy and respect. After all, we're not going to hurt each other, are we? Beef was plentiful at our house. Having no chickens available prompted Chief to rig up an incubator-like home for biddies. He furnished an old army trunk with a light bulb and thermometer to assure correct temperature. Neither of us had lived with chickens. The trunk was in our dining area.

Our first dinner party was the last. After chasing to behead, dunking in hot water to defeather, and all that cooking, we took the "never-again" pledge. Chief announced to his army buddies, "If you want chicken, you'll have to chase, behead, and clean them Saturday afternoon. I'll furnish the drinks and ball game. Libbylove will cook." These were radio days. Quite a picture—all that neckringing, fingers filled with wet feathers. All that was forgotten as their favorite team made a touchdown. Saturday afternoon fever. Away from familiar stadiums, football still raged. Chief made it all fun.

After chicken preparations, the men left, returning later in the evening with their wives, spruced up for a Saturday night out. Our love nest was headquarters. We were the only couple in our gang with children. Sometimes we put our two babies to bed at a friend's house, the hostess for the evening. We'd go over later, all dressed up. After the party we collected the sleepyheads, moved playpens, and all the gear home. This was when I discovered, "You can sleep an hour longer on Sunday morning." I put a few surprises in the children's bed after they were sound asleep. Cloth books worked fine, a banana wasn't too messy, crackers great. A cold bottle of milk was the right temperature when they awakened. This kept them quietly occupied a precious hour.

Churches had no nurseries then. Chief and I took turns going to church. We still had the family Bible and our faith. It was evergrowing. We still felt most blessed. Twice I had taken pictures and curtains down, waiting for the packers. Twice they were put back, orders canceled. "You can't take my dentist!" Twice the dentists assigned to these overseas duties were lost at the bottom of the ocean. They went down with their bombarded ships. We were always conscious the dear Lord spared us, and we were extremely grateful.

After World War II, back in Carolina, safe and sound, Chief and I pitched our tent at my Mom's. It was an interim arrangement while he looked for an office and wigwam of our own. I enjoyed built-in sitters for our two children.

Number three was on the way. I enjoyed being with my Mom. All of us basked in grandparenting love. Our faith was strengthened by our return to the church we were married in, enjoying once more Christian fellowship. There were tears this time of thanksgiving to be safely home.

Chief dubbed the wigwam we purchased "a psychiatric saltbox." Typical starter house. It was so small. He swore if you didn't need a psychiatrist when you moved in, you would before you moved out. My nesting instincts were satisfied. I painted guardian angels over the children's beds. Their creative instincts were satisfied. They dug a hole in the backyard. A good rain, with a little help from the water hose, provided an ideal swimming pool. They moved the sliding board to an advantageous position. It became the high dive. The picnic table became the low dive. The neighbors took a dim view of the whole operation. It was off limits to some children.

Our small fry were the envy of their friends. A quick check with our pediatrician reassured us: "Children will not meet a quick demise by playing in muddy water." Fortunately, the novelty soon wore off. In fact, the charm didn't last half as long as the highway system they built with readymix concrete. More fascinating than the Indianapolis Speedway, more complex than the Los Angeles Freeway. Completely ignored by their mom, Libbylove.

You can't say no to life. I always felt no's discouraged creativity, ideas, and learning experiences. I tried to keep them at a minimum. Our fenced-in backyard was the scene of constant activity. The picnic table groaned from the weight of children, hammers, and nails. It was turned alternatively from an airplane to covered wagon as need be. I felt a kindred spirit with Mrs. Conant, the mother of Dr. James Bryant Conant, scientist and educator. This mother admitted her house and yard were the scene of many childish experiments. I tried to allow these little cocoons freedom to blossom in their own unique way. Children are our precious gifts from God. I attempted to guide them very prayerfully.

We outgrew our Psychiatric Saltbox house when child #4—#3 son—came. There was no getting away from each other. Chief found a big fifty-year-old house. Everything was spacious. A front porch was good for rainy-day bike riding. The entrance hall was extra wide from front to back door. High ceilings. Four fireplaces up and downstairs. It was great to stretch out. Beside the usual rooms were bonuses like a butler's pantry, ironing room, breakfast room, den, and children's playroom with adjoining bathroom on the first floor. Upstairs, the hall was the same size as the entrance hall, large enough to stash away extra guests on daybeds. A large master bedroom, bedroom for child #1—daughter #1—plus an oversized bunk room for the boys with walk-in closets gave us much-needed privacy. An extra bedroom boasted a lavatory. It became the guest room or "sickroom" when necessary.

The yard was enclosed by a six-foot fence. It hid the children's interesting projects. There were lots of old trees to stretch out under, where they could read or be read to, and there was room for ball games. The main attraction was an old two-story barn. It became everything from club headquarters to a firehouse. This Trinity Avenue home was called "Trinity Treat."

Trinity Treat was to be a ten-year plan. Close to church, ball parks, and schools. What a treat to be able to walk to activities. Not only did we enjoy more room, but it enabled us to have more house guests. The word gets around. Once, while making bed check, I missed our eldest son. I looked in the guest room, thinking he was tired of bunk-bed living. He was in the double bed. Beside him was a hulk completely covered by the bedspread. No breathing room. I sped down the hall to enlist Chief to investigate. After all, chiefs are brave. The hulk turned out to be the 220-pound halfback son of an out-of-town friend. His grandparents lived down the street, and their house was overloaded.

Chief cleared up that mystery before we went to sleep. Usually we had to wait until morning to solve most of them. The suspense was and is terrible. We have a rule. Never awaken anyone. Never. Only if the house is afire. Sleep is hard to come by. If someone is asleep, believe me, they need it.

I'll never forget the night Chief and I were preparing for bed. He asked me if we had a bird. I assured him I had done animal count right after bed count. No bird. He declared there was a bird cage in the upstairs hall. There *was* a bird cage, but it contained two little white mice. It was difficult to wait for the morning explanation.

The seven-year-old confessed with none of the usual, "I don't know." His teacher asked for a "mice sitter" over the weekend, so my son volunteered. There was nothing I could say when he turned those blue eyes my way, declaring, "You always said, Mom, that our home is open to everyone"; especially when he added the clincher, "Remember if you do it unto the least of . . . something like that."

True. There has always been room in our home. The accommodations are not predictable, the built-in entertainment likewise. Some friends reluctantly let their offspring visit. They claimed it took their children too long to recuperate. The excitement was too much for them. I know the feeling.

Quiet time is respected at our house. They never outgrew it. It mattered not if they sleep, read, or daydream, quiet time is a requirement. Alone in your ivory tower. It might be their own room, in a tree camp, or under the dining room table. They learned to adjust to one another. I also wanted them to get acquainted with themselves, their own secret thoughts. I wanted them to discover it is possible to be by yourself—but never be alone. Our Heavenly Father is always with us. Right beside us. Not thousands of years ago. Right now. This very minute.

Trinity Treat was perfect for our big family. Our next-door neighbor, a church, started campaigning to buy our property. They needed it for parking. They enlarged the church. All kinds of forbidden building materials were piled temptingly near. My duties were enlarged to include security and police work, not to mention safety. We had to admit our ten-year plan was cut to five. The time was right for building our own dream house.

We chose a wooded area with streams to dam, camps to make, and tree houses to build. No more traffic. No more car doors opening, children being dumped outside my door—other folks' children. No more close calls as children crossed busy streets. We reluctantly left Trinity Treat.

We lovingly named our new home "Bedlam." It seemed appropriate for headquarters for the eleven of us. Bedlam doesn't have high ceilings or many hiding places, but it does have more bathrooms. The floors are vinyl tile. No more mopping spilled milk from hardwood floors. Only the living room boasts wooden floors and Persian carpets. Absolutely nothing shows on these beauties. Childproof.

It is difficult to describe the decor of a large family home. It ranges from disaster to lived-in. The entrance hall should look inviting. The table is hidden by the daily collection of "don't forget's." Books, jackets, and sports gear have a way of shifting and moving all over the house. I noted the collection of treasures one day to be taken to school. Average. A small snake, a bumblebee in a coffee can, some seaweed, and sea shells.

Bedlam's kitchen fascinates some folks. I saw nothing

unusual about stainless steel fixtures, oversized cooking utensils, shades of my hotel-home days. A restaurant-sized grill for hamburgers or pancakes is a must. A crock pot becomes a twenty-five pound sugar container. Decorative casserole dishes serve twenty-four. Always casseroles. They stretch to accommodate the open-door policy.

There are scads of cookbooks. Especially foreign cookbooks. They have the knack of making something out of nothing. I use them to prepare a meal characteristic of the country a child is studying. Calling a vegetable by a foreign name is pretty sneaky. I admit I have. The troops relished many foods before they discovered they weren't supposed to like them; they had eaten zucchini for years before they knew it was squash. By then, they were hooked.

The attic looks like a department store. That's where we keep the hand-me-downs: clothes, costumes, start for newlyweds, abandoned furniture, and cooking utensils. Our attic has such a widespread reputation the local television station calls to borrow for their commercials. Where else can you find a forgotten porkpie hat or black derby? Whatever the style, I'm ready.

The basement of Bedlam is the neighborhood YMCA. Afternoons it is full of children. There's Ping-Pong and pool. Some work on their scientific experiments. Others build or dismantle an abandoned TV. One plays his set of drums. The basement, like the attic, is the length and width of the house. A cold-drink box, complete with money slot, provides refreshments—at a price. The perfect solution for me. We keep it filled with drinks. The machine looks better. No more drinks tucked into window sills, squirreled away in drawers. The money has to be earned. The profit is used to recover the pool table with felt. Or buy Ping-Pong balls. Another basement innovation is a telephone booth. A necessary installation. It is impossible to hear over the basement phone most of the time.

Everything in Bedlam is chipped, split, or nicked. The dining-room table is five feet wide. It seats fourteen comfortably. The only trouble is, if you don't have both ham and turkey, it looks bare. I cherish the chairs. They still have baby teeth marks on their backs. The walls are filled with pictures, needlework, and signs. The troops say if I don't know what to do with something, I hang it on the wall.

An art major in college, I live with my paintings. Can't part with my mementos of fun times or gifts from friends and family. The sign, "Welcome to Bedlam," greets you in the entrance hall. It's one of many signs we have collected over the years. Chief's favorite uses a bit of reverse psychology. "May your heart and your house always be too small for your friends." Believe me, Bedlam's seams stretch lovingly to accommodate all who enter.

> . . . given to hospitality (Rom. 12:13*b*).
> Well reported of for good works; if she have brought up children, if she have lodged strangers, if she have washed the saints' feet, if she have relieved the afflicted, if she have diligently followed every good work (1 Tim. 5:10).

6
All in a Mother's Line of Duty
(or Forty Winks Under the Sink)

The croupy cough of the baby called me out of bed on the run. Fear raced through my body. Quickly I found my bedroom shoes, couldn't get my feet into them, so I pushed them aside. Bending down to put them on was out of the question since an eight-month pregnancy stood in the way. Charging down the hall, I was completely unaware of my clumsiness. Noting the baby's flushed face, I listened carefully to his breathing. Unmistakably croup.

I assembled the vaporizer, waiting for its reassuring hissing sound. Nothing happened. A glance at the clock, 3:30 AM, convinced me this was no time to borrow a neighbor's vaporizer. Hot plate? No. It was on the blink too. What now?

I adjusted a slow stream of hot water in the tub. Steam was rising—a lovely sight. I carefully closed the door behind me as I went to get the baby. I didn't want a bit of that lovely mist to escape. After hurrying back to the bathroom with my baby protectively snuggled in my arms, I settled myself smugly on the "throne," the only seat in the place. In my joy over the steam, I was oblivious of myself or the other unseen baby I was carrying. Things began to become crowded all around. This spacious bathroom seemed smaller and smaller. My joy soon turned to personal discomfort, aided by arms suddenly leaden. Not to be daunted, with my baby still in my arms, off to the bedroom I went to pull and tug an old rocker into the bathroom.

At the threshold of the bathroom door, I faced another problem. I could get the rocker in the doorway but couldn't close the door. All this time precious steam was escaping. Glancing at the baby, I was reminded he didn't need sudden temperature changes.

The dragging, banging noises awakened Chief. He wandered sleepily down the hall to inquire disinterestedly "What's the matter?" I plopped the baby in his arms as I related my predicament. He surveyed the situation. True to his sex, he came up with an immediate solution.

"Move the baby's bed into the bathroom. He can sleep and so can you."

I weakly protested. I pointed out my rocking-chair misfit. After a comforting "we're-in-this-together" look, he went to get the baby bed. I fled with the baby back to the steaming bathroom. I again perched on the "throne." I tried to arrange myself and the babies to give Chief every available inch to move the bed around in. I admired his muscles as I watched him use the same angle getting in as I did with the rocker. With the strength and foresight of a male, he easily lifted the bed up and over the lavatory directly left of the door. With bed poised high in the air, he swung it over the tub and pushed the door shut with his foot as he swung the bed down into the only available space—a perfect fit directly behind the bathroom door, in front of the linen closet door.

The bed filled the bathroom completely. I was still ensconced on my "throne," baby in arms, away from the line of fire. Chief left with a triumphant grin. It wasn't easy. He barely managed to squeeze between the lavatory and bed. Somehow he closed the door. All the time he was sending me reassuring messages.

". . . As soon as the baby's asleep come on to bed. He'll be okay. We'll check on him." He was using that term "we" loosely, of course.

Comforted again, I reminded myself how fortunate I was to have an understanding spouse. I sent many "thank you's" to my Heavenly Father. I happily settled the baby in his bed; checked the tub to be sure it would not run over. I thought about my own warm bed. I made an immediate horrible discovery: *I couldn't get out of the bathroom!*

There was enough room for me to slide between the tub and bed if I turned my front side toward the tub. I couldn't get my big frame between the bed and the lavatory. I couldn't crawl under the bed. I sat back down on the "throne." I looked down at my eight-month pregnancy. I surveyed the situation dismally.

You can't beat brains and education. *There must be a solution,* I thought. I walked the narrow path between the tub and bed to try to open the door. This feat entailed balancing precariously on the rim of the tub with one foot, leaning on the lavatory with my right elbow, while my free foot swung in the air. I managed to open the bathroom door.

I gave my best "fish wife" yell. It eventually brings the small fry from the hinterlands. No results. Still trembling in this awkward position, I gave my "all hands on deck, P.D.Q." (D. for doggone) yell. Still no results. I screamed, "Help, murder, police!" Still nothing. I had had it. I let loose language learned at my father's knee. My vocabulary was still colorful though limited. Absolutely no results!

I was so mad by this time, I could effortlessly shift my weight—one hundred and plenty—to the other side. I wrapped my arm around the baby bed, used the other arm to open the medicine cabinet. Still on my dangerous perch, I pulled out the largest thing I could find. I flung it down the hall. Clank! Clank! In my right mind, I would check its price before being so reckless. Not tonight. I was thoroughly mad.

I listened intently. A mocking veil of silence lay over the old house, Trinity Treat—a house usually jumping and creaking joyfully. Completely defeated, depressed and dog-tired, I trembled down from my station. I dragged myself back to my "throne." It was beginning to feel like home.

I weakly fought the waves of self-pity that flowed over me. Self-pity is one luxury I don't allow myself. I thought I was entitled to a moment and I took it.

Then the Heavenly Nudge. *Okay! Okay!* I marched myself into a mental corner and talked with my Heavenly Father.

"Listen here," He said, "Quit complaining. Partying 'til dawn doesn't tire you. Why should mothering till dawn wear you out? The baby's fine. The other children are fine. Chief's fine. You're the problem. Where is your sense of humor?"

"Okay. Okay," I answered. "So it's hilarious. I'll laugh tomorrow, Dear Lord. I am tired."

"You only make yourself more tired. Relax. Find joy. It is not the end of the world. It is an adventure. You can stand anything that is temporary. Remember? I am always with you. Trust Me. Relax."

By another contortionist act, I opened the linen closet door at the foot of the bed. I started pulling out towels to make a pallet. I bunched more towels for a pillow. At least my full middle was free. My legs were under the baby's bed. When I opened my eyes, I could see the underneath part of the lavatory. I preferred to shut them.

Not bad. I always claimed to like hard beds.

Finally, appreciating the amusement of the situation, I gratefully fell asleep, murmuring, "Thank you, Dear Lord. One more time."

All too soon I was awakened by banging on the door. The

underside of the lavatory didn't look any better by daylight. The banging persisted. I could barely reach the doorknob. I turned it. Through the cracked doorway I could see a pair of little feet. My effort to get up and out from under the bed and sink is indescribable.

"Mama. What are you doing under that bed? I've got to use the bathroom!"

My middle child easily slipped between the bed and lavatory.

"Mama, I don't see why you slept under the baby bed," he confided as he went to the bathroom.

Then and there I demonstrated my inability to escape. He rushed out to spread the news.

"Come see Mama! Come see Mama!"

The old house sprung to life. Little feet sped down the hall to view the prison dear Mama was in. All the running and giggling brought Chief to the scene.

"Really, Libbylove, what you won't do for a laugh. What are you doing under that bed? Why didn't you come to our bed?"

All these questions before he fully comprehended. Then he gave me his snow-melting smile. "Of all things," Chief chuckled.

I couldn't resist the ludicrous situation. I joined the laughter of my crew, trying to act indignant, declaring, "Why don't you sell tickets?"

The baby eagerly awaited arms to lift him out of bed. I excitedly waited for the bed to be maneuvered up over the lavatory out into the hall. I had been in prison long enough.

I sent up more silent "Thank you, Dear Lord's" while hamming it up by singing, "I'm Just a Prisoner of Love!"

7
The Sunday Special
(or Here We Go, Ready or Not!)

The Sunday Special leaves our house at a quarter of ten every Sunday morning. Ready or not. If you don't make it aboard, you can expect punishment. This Special is made up of two cars. Their destination is church. Sunday school and church are command performances.

The first car takes the ushers and Sunday school teachers, the second car carries the stragglers and me. I'm the mama of this crew. All mamas are stragglers. With nine children, two cars are a necessity. We don't own a Greyhound bus.

Think of me on Sunday: the mother of this crew, the original whirling dervish with definite top-sergeant characteristics. As the commanding general sleeps lightly before a battle, so do I on Saturday nights. I know what's facing me Sunday morning. Unclothed, unfed offsprings—my troops. Since attendance at church is compulsory, nothing short of illness keeps you away. Even then you go through the service at home using the Bible as a guide. There are hymns, too.

Picture lost shoes. Always lost shoes. Regardless of the different plans I can devise, there are always lost shoes. An older child is assigned to polishing the footwear on Saturday night. I even tried lining up the gleaming shoes, pair-by-pair, at the foot of the stairs, out of the traffic. I dared anyone to remove them.

Next morning I was pleased to note all shoes accounted for. After breakfast they took them to their rooms. Bless pat if the three-year-old didn't lose a shoe en route. We looked everywhere. Turned the room, including the mattress, upside down. Not to be outdone, I brought out my bag of old shoes. I buy them alike for this reason. We found one for the three-year-old culprit. It was the same type shoe but the wrong size! Picture him, dragging one foot, dragging down the aisle of the church. The shoe was so large he dared not lift his foot off the floor lest he might lose it. Sometimes we have the opposite problem. The shoe is too small. Then they limp down the aisle.

Limping or dragging, they still go. If not, he is campused for the rest of the day. Only sickness is a forgiveable excuse. The punishment is worse on a sunny day. Maybe it seems that way because I am the jailer. I try hard to make sure that they get to the church on time.

Sunday mornings we are long on religion and short on breakfast. That's the only morning I don't serve a big meal. Sundays we have hot or cold cereal, according to the season; doughnuts and milk, according to the time; bananas en route, if pressed for time. My crew thinks of this as a snack. After church they're starved and rather vocal. We charge to the nearest hot dog place to fill up since the whole bunch can eat cheaply and quickly. The gorging tides everyone over until big mealtime later in the day. For me it is a short rest from the nerve-wracking journey to church.

Our dessert is a cone of ice cream, quite a ceremony. It involves Chief patiently waiting for everyone to think about the flavor one wants. Chief pretends to remember each and every request, ranging from raspberry parfait to coffee ice cream. Each child wants something different. Chief comes back loaded down with *all* chocolate or *all* vanilla or *all* cherry—*whatever flavor Chief wants.* They know this will happen and start laughing when he comes into sight. They enjoy the surprise. Chief claims they don't know what they want anyway, that thinking about it is the most fun.

After we reach home, the breakfast debris is cleared away. All hands on deck accomplish this feat. Then each one goes his separate way. Some play the sport of their choice; others read or catch up on their studies. The little ones and mama nap. I have my sign, "At home, Sunday afternoons from two to four. Hope you are the same," prominently displayed on the basement door.

Mama is on call, however, to referee fights, help with the homework, discuss problems, or nurse the sick. Not everyone knows about my sign. The Southern custom of Sunday afternoon visiting still prevails. You have to be ready for that possibility.

One Sunday afternoon was unusually hectic. I was trying to rest my usual pregnant self. The teenagers were playing pool. The preschoolers were riding their trikes around the table. The in-betweens were watching TV. Rock and roll music blared forth from somewhere. Bombarded by these sounds, I was fast reaching the explosion point.

The day was rainy. I thought I was stupid to stay home. I had built-in baby sitters. My youngest was peacefully sleeping, so I lured the trike riders upstairs. I told them they could ride around the dining room table—usually off limits —I was desperate. I invited the wrestlers upstairs to resume their matches on the living room Oriental rugs. Even though I moved furniture out of the way, they eyed me suspiciously. They proceeded cautiously with their holds. The teenagers were jubilant in the basement, undisturbed by small fry.

I'm not taking up for Sunday golf, but Chief went to the golf course. It was pouring down. Nothing interferes with his golf games—rain, sleet, wind, even snow. Then they paint the golf balls red.

After leaving my phone number in several so-called reliable hands, I fled to the nearby clubhouse. I found a comfortable corner chair to fall into. The place was empty on Sunday afternoon. The peace and quiet flowed over me. The only sound was soft rain sliding down the big picture window. A couple, an older pair who had no children, wandered in. They took one long look at this pregnant woman alone in this big room in the early afternoon. They seemed perplexed.

"Won't you join us?" they graciously asked.

When I declined, I could tell they were worried. They whispered a while and then gazed at me. A few minutes later, they asked me to join them for a bite to eat. Again, I declined. They began to stir around in their seats. I could read their thoughts . . . *bound to have domestic problems. Children? Husband?* They both got up and came over. It was more than I could stand. Even though I knew they could not understand I tried to give them a verbal picture of my household on a rainy Sunday afternoon.

They politely listened. I tried to convince them I was happy. I emphasized the joy in peace and quiet. These feelings seemed foreign to them. I didn't want to ruin their day. I joined them. I admit the adult conversation was great. The food refreshed me. The chore of cooking supper, the big meal of the day, seemed small.

I felt foolish as I sped home. "Dear Father, I know You don't give us any more than we can take. I certainly asked for it. With Your help, I can make it. Thank You for Your blessings. All nine of them."

After Sunday afternoon spent doing your own thing, we gather for togetherness around the dining room table. Because it's impossible to reach across the five-foot table, I serve the plates. Unsteady little hands and dripping food doesn't help anyone. We exchange stories of the day. Even I had one that night. The "Goodness, Mom, we're sorry" made me feel even more foolish to escape my prison of love. At least I proved to myself I had an out. Since I had an option, I felt more content.

Every topic of table conversation has to be of general interest. That's a chore in itself. This is one of the few meals we have family hour. The rest of the week is filled with ball practice, music, Scouts, or meetings. As Earl Wilson put it, "The American home has everything in it but the family." We look forward to our Sunday worship and fellowship together.

I look forward to bedtime. Following the work chart, one child does the dishes, another puts the little ones to bed, another feeds the animals, all working together until their chores are done. I try to keep this show on the road. It is good training that pays off when I am indisposed. They can run the show without me.

The new week starts on Sunday. They consult the chore chart for the change of duties. The one with breakfast for the week plans the morning meal. He gathers all the ingredients, writes the menu on the blackboard for me, rouses the family next morning while I cook, and helps me put the breakfast on the table.

The Sunday night duties over with, I hit the sack while Chief naps in front of the TV. An avid reader, I anticipate a leisurely evening. Unless company calls, I fall asleep before reading two lines! It is a happy, peaceful sleep of a commanding general after battle. With the memory of my family taking up the front pew at church, like James I say again and again, "I count it all joy!" (see Jas. 1:2).

8
December 26th
(or Chaos at the Griffins)

The day after Christmas all through the house every creature is stirring. Except me! My spirit is in good shape but my flesh is mighty weak. I'm a coward. I'm not ready to face the old routine—tears that accompany new broken toys. I would like to bask in the warm memory of Christmas Day and its excitement. No way. The day after Christmas is an anticlimactic slump. The slump is me and has nothing to do with whether I was expecting a baby or just had one. It's just no fun facing children with broken toys.

So there have been some rather hectic days after Christmas at our house.

One of the most memorable days started when I was awakened by somebody who kept chanting, "The pony's gone. The pony's gone."

"Santa" had brought us a pony—just what we needed with nine kids, a dog, cat, kittens, of course, and a parakeet. We thought Santa had made a mistake. Nobody had asked for a pony. Santa is like that at our house, though. He brings what he wants us to have.

The poor mantle on that Christmas Eve couldn't endure one more tack hole, so down to the basement playroom went the tree and stockings. Each child selects a chair or bench for their loot. His or her stocking with the child's name on it designates each one's own receiving station.

The pony was a family affair, so he was tied outside the basement door. The rope had slipped off his neck this morning after Christmas. The little beast had wandered away at 6:00 AM Chief and I were conducting a contest to see who could out-pretend being asleep.

We had already told child #1—girl #1—now eighteen, goodbye. She just had to fly to Washington with her boyfriend and his father. They were to bring back an airplane. They'd be back for lunch.

The chant continued, kept getting louder. "The pony's down the street. The pony's down the street."

Talk about passing the buck. The chore of retrieving the pony had been passed from the six-year-old to the thirteen-year-old. It was fast going up the line of command.

When the pony wandered out of our yard, up the street, onto the golf course, hallowed ground, that did arouse a response from Chief. He had visions of damages to be paid. The most drastic steps were taken. We then tried to wake up our seventeen-year-old (#2 child—#1 son).

Have you tried waking up a seventeen-year-old boy lately? It isn't easy. He finally stumbled sleepily up to the golf course with our shouting encouragement all the way—"You're bigger than the pony!"

By this time, Chief and I had completely given up our contest of pretending sleep. We admitted it couldn't be done with nine kids around. After a breakfast we don't remember, Chief escaped to town to buy supplies to build a pony stall. I stashed child #9 in the car with him. I never believe in letting a handsome father out of the house without a chaperone. A two-year-old isn't much help anyway.

I had to swig another cup of coffee to get fortified for the main event, a birthday party. Child #7—girl #2—the December twenty-sixth baby, had never had a birthday party. She was six today. The whole family agreed she was going to have a party.

My brood never wanted birthday parties. They live in a crowd. Their idea of a treat is to get off by themselves with their parents. They made an exception of girl #2. She had been to so many birthday parties. Now it was her turn.

I had to rearrange my usual strategy. I had no outside help that day. Chief had gone shopping, my older helpers busy (one flown to Washington, one pony chasing). So I delegated child #3—son #2—to sweep the basement, scene of the party; child #4—son #3—to clean the living room (we party all over the house); and child #5—son #4—to clean the back porch. Children 6, 7, and 8 were step-and-fetch-its. I supervised this burst of activity, all dedicated to birthday girl. Real active togetherness.

By this time child #1—daughter #1—had returned from Washington. Just in time. Her boyfriend saddled the pony. This brought his stock up in the family.

All too soon the eighteen six-year-old girls arrived. They brought birthday presents along with their Christmas dolls. They were ready for the "Pony-Doll Tea Party." After throwing down coats, piling their dolls alongside, with presents flying everywhere, they dashed to the front yard. Each wanted to be the first to ride the pony—the main attraction.

All hands were on deck. The boyfriend was pressed into leading the squealing pony riders around the front yard. Child #1—daughter #1—beamed her approval. What muscles. What lamb-like cooperativeness. Children #2 and #3 went to help Chief unload supplies to build a pony stall. Chief enlisted two or three teenagers who wandered by, entranced with all the action around our house. Tempers, nails, and hammers flew in the backyard. Pony riding in the front. Refreshment fixing inside.

Chief's two sisters appeared on the scene. One had her

three-year-old son with her—and both brought their dogs. These two canines, added to those of the teenage carpenters built up the collection. It looked like a dog party as well as a pony party.

Not being able to stand idleness, I poked a camera into one sister's hand. She was declared official photographer for the day. I dragged the other sister with me. We set the dining room table with tea sets for the little girls and their dolls. It took all the tea sets in our collection, plus those "Santa" brought to do the job. It was fun.

When the parents came to claim their children, there was a mad scramble. Trying to match the right doll to the right child to the right coat wasn't easy. I shouted encouragement, "Here's her doll. Here's her coat." After a while I changed it to, "Don't worry about the dolls and coats, friends. Just be sure to get your children."

It was well worth the effort to see the joyful countenance of birthday girl. It made my hurting feet and shaky nerves feel a heap better. The thought of a holiday party to which Chief and I were invited, later in the day, helped immeasurably, too.

A big pot of soup, simmering on the stove, was pulled to the front line. Child #3—son #2—was the commander of battle of the bed. Child #1, daughter #1 was at her boyfriend's home for dinner. Child #2, son #1 went to a basketball game. Child #4 was babysitting for a neighbor; Child #5 was enjoying a bingo party. A quiet evening awaited Child #3, built-in sitter, left with only #'s 6, 7, 8, and 9!

Chief and I were so late for the party we missed all the food and adult conversation. We went next door for food—starved. A rare treat of a leisurely meal lowered our blood pressure to normal. Also our perspective. We then took off to see a bedridden friend. So blessed are we!

We put our tired bodies to bed—soothed by the memory of all our children in their red night clothes. Yesterday morning had been Christmas morning! It seemed so long ago. They were waiting for our signal to see their loot. When it came, instead of pushing each other down the stairs, remember what they did? I never could forget! They lustily but reverently sang, "Happy Birthday, Dear Jesus!" as they slowly went downstairs. They were not prompted nor rehearsed—it was their idea. That memory stays with me through the years!

9
The "Meanest Mamas' Club"
(or The Last of the Red Hot Mamas)

When does the "Meanest Mamas Club" meet? I have a prospective member. Saw her in the supermarket. She was restraining her child from pulling down the stock. Do you have a chapter in your town? You probably do and don't know it.

How can you identify members? By their looks, if you're discerning. They have calloused, elephant-hide skins acquired from years of dodging hurled invectives: "I hate you! You're the Meanest Mama!" Others have seal skin from constant whines and tears sliding off their back and huge rabbit ears from years of " . . . but *everybody,* just everybody but *me*!"

Meanest Mamas' ears are very sensitive (see Prov. 15:31). Especially when trying to head off potential trouble for their offspring. These tuned-in individuals don't miss a trick. Their peripheral vision is pluperfect. They have eyes in the backs of their heads (see Prov. 15:3). Added to the anterior eyes, nothing escapes them. Members have overdeveloped arms from much exercise (see Prov. 31:17)—gained by some spankings (Prov. 29:15), a lot of restraining (see Prov. 29:17) and tons of hugging (see 1 John 4:19). Meanest Mamas have soft, springy feet. They sneak upstairs to placate an unhappy child (see 2 Cor. 1:4), medicate the sick (see Jas. 5:15), or reassure the frightened (see Isa. 35:4).

In addition to their peculiar physical characteristics, Meanest Mamas' grooming is odd. Yesterday #1 child—#1 girl—asked why mamas look so rumpled and soiled. I gave her so many *for instances,* she'll never ask again. Not this Mean Mama.

"Five minutes is not enough dressing time. The older you get, the longer it takes to gild the lily."

That's all the time I have, slinging a cake in the oven before the next carpool. Meanest Mamas think children will remember cake odors more fondly than Chanel #5. It isn't easy to stay neat while trying to keep little ones from falling into the batter. They perch precariously around and over the mixing bowl. After removing cake dough from under fingernails, the nail polish is missing. Can't fix the nails. Someone borrowed the polish to label something or used it to paint chigger bites.

Meanest Mamas rarely return to a mirror after the morning look. The fate of lipsticks is probably universal. Gone the way of face creams and magic markers. On walls. Lately my comb was missing. Child #7—daughter #2—used it to comb her dolly's hair. No hairbrush. A budding swain usurped it? No, it was used to groom the dog! Manicured, meticulous Meanest Mamas? Never.

I saw a likely Meanest Mama yesterday. She had the inevitable smelly white spot on the shoulder of her dress. Anyone who can learn the secret of removing spilled milk can unlock the secrets of the world. Nothing removes or camouflages it. Understanding smiles of Meanest Mamas help. Not much. To the member, spilled milk spots are a badge of honor. It proves their babies are cuddled and loved. The ring of smudgy spots around the dress hemline is nothing to ridicule like "ring around the collar." It shows a child sought and was given love and comfort. It shows a chastised one held to receive forgiveness (Eph. 4:32).

Meanest Mamas come in all sizes and shapes. Some skinny—not taking time to eat. Some fat—can't remember eating. All have big mouths. They're always moving, sometimes refereeing—"Mama, *he* started it!" "No, *she* started it!" (see 2 Sam. 15:4); sympathizing—"Don't believe it, but I was your age once" (see Prov. 15:23); encouraging—"You'll get over it before you get married!" (see Prov. 15:30); preaching—"If I don't try to teach you right from wrong, who will?"; explaining—"You're not *everybody.* You're you. Not your brother. Sister. Friend. You." (see Eph. 2:10).

These mouths can cajole, persuade, amuse, irritate, or explode. Carving names on furniture with pins does light this Meanest Mama's fuse. Teething marks on dining room chairs are treasured—a different matter entirely.

Meanest Mamas aren't popular, sought-after or necessarily adored. They're just necessary. Whistler's mom was painted with her hands in her lap. Meanest Mamas rarely sit. Never with folded hands. Chasing a vanishing culprit one afternoon, my #2 child—#1 son's—friend, eyeballed me. He shook his head, announcing, "Never underestimate a little woman. She's worse than a top sergeant!" My son advised him to be quiet. Meanest Mamas dish out rules and regulations to any child in the household, visitors or not. Justice for all (see Prov. 29:15,17).

Where do you find Meanest Mamas? Home or grocery generally. Hole-in-the-head ones can be found at Scout meetings. Brawny, faithful ones are holding up the pillars of the church. Those with extra high pain tolerance are enduring P.T.A. meetings. The road runners are chauffering carpools to music and lessons of all kinds. Mature Meanest Mamas can be seen fiddling nervously outside athletic fields, waiting to pick up budding ball players, while dinner burns.

The Meanest Mamas Club is exclusive. It excludes complaining females who make mama noises, or braggarts who crow as if they invented motherhood. They blackball husband-snipers and martyrs-to-motherhood. Members in good standing resist pressure from kids, from indecisive parents who refuse to accept the duties of parenthood, who try to con others into doing their parental chores, from parents who can't take a stand and stick by it, who ignore the Good Book.

Each Meanest Mama has her own witches' brew recipe. Some demand a portion of respect for themselves and others. Some teach lessons based on the Golden Rule—private property; free enterprise; with rights come responsibilities. Some mix strange potions of no-TV weeknights, curfew for too-young-to-be-out age, insistence on good manners, kindness and consideration for others. Their theme song is, "I love you."

Meanest Mamas have stubborn traits. This Meanest Mama doesn't do children's homework or children's household chores. Doesn't make excuses or lie for them. Doesn't take their left-at-home books or lunches to school. Believes in cause and effect. If you make a mess, clean it up. You make your own bed, lie in it. What you sow, you reap. (see Gal. 6:7). Thinks everyone is entitled to make their own mistakes—and pay for them. It's a two-way street. Rules are the same for parents and children. She knows the meaning of these rarely heard words—*duty, responsibility, self-discipline.* She takes her text from the Bible (see Prov. 2:6).

Meanest Mamas become Red Hot Mamas when riled: fighting to keep their childrens' names from being sold to porn pusher's lists; trying to stave off evil influences and outside pressures as long as possible; teaching them to assemble and wear their own protective armor (see Eph. 6:11); constantly alerting them to biased news and biased people; introducing them to Rocks to build on (see Ps. 18:2, 92:15).

Always listening (see 1 Sam 3:10). Always loving (see John 15:12,17; Ps. 63:3).

Are there rewards for Meanest Mamas? Each has her own. Sometimes there's an unexpected admission. Once I heard mine whisper, "I'm glad you're not like other mothers!" Another time I caught an admiring glance when I was clowning around, hamming it up to make a point. #2 child —#1 son—feigned indignance, "You mean I'll be like *that* when I grow up!" I enjoyed overhearing #3 child—#2 son—brag, not complain, "Sure thing my mama wouldn't let me do that!"

You can tell when you're making progress. Child #4—son #3—was diligently studying his Sunday School lesson. He noticed a middle-aged midget riding a bicycle, smoking a long cigar. Never saw a midget before, thought he was a boy.

"Mom, look at that boy smoking that cigar!" He shook his head disgustedly. "He ought to be ashamed, breaking the Lord's Commandment!"

My imagination took off. I had tried to explain each of the Ten Commandments. I was stumped.

"Which commandment is he breaking, son?"

"Oh, you know, Mom," he said, "Thou shalt not commit adultery."

"How's that?" I asked, not quite understanding—scared to ask.

"You know, children going around trying to act like *adults!*"

In retrospect you do wonder how adults appear to children—especially Meanest Mamas to their children's friends. You can tell. It must be okay. Our house stays full of them. You're the one they ask to chaperone or be the leader. Maybe they want to see what you'll do next. No. Maybe they like being around childish adults. Sometimes you have to listen. They'll tell you.

On a Girl Scout campout, I finished helping Brownies bed down under the stars. I was trying to get some shuteye. I rearranged my tired body to avoid the sharp stobs of cut corn stalks. I was miserable. Uncomfortable. No amount of toothbrushing could rid my mouth of the sand from eating "biscuits on a stick." Why is it always windy on these outings? I'm really too old for roughing it!

"Mrs. G.! Mrs. G!"

What could they possibly want this time?

"Thanks for bringing us. My Mom's scared of everything. The dark! Bugs! She wouldn't come."

Smart woman, I thought. *Not wasting a beautiful moonlit night sleeping between corn rows. Alone.*

"Yeah, thanks, Mrs. G.," another voice chimed in. "You're making *everything* fun!"

"Cut it out, girls. Blarney will get you nowhere. I'm too tired to stumble through sleeping bags. Praise improves my hearing. Can you hear this? A kiss for each of you!"

Ten loud smacks were greeted by applause and a round of, "For she's a jolly good fellow!" Rewards? Yes, in my book.

Like most Meanest Mamas, I'm a sucker for praise. I stuck with those Brownies right on up to Senior Scouts. Any sign of learning, any sign of real interest spurred me on. If they were willing to give up an afternoon a week during high school, so was I. Rewards? How about this one?

After a Scout meeting, I was waiting outside the restroom to chauffer some of them home. They all filed out grinning. My #1 child—#1 girl—was shaking her head, laughing the hardest.

"Mom, you won't believe!"

"Try me." Not listening, really. Thinking of the little ones at home that needed some of my attention.

"They just voted you the mom they'd love to have!"

I checked my daughter's face. Approval. Hard to hug ten girls at once. I forgot all about the difficulty of dividing myself in so many pieces. Only Meanest Mamas with their overdeveloped arms could manage hugging ten at a time. Rewards? You can't buy those (see Eccl. 7:1; 11:1).

When does the Meanest Mama's Club meet again? I wouldn't miss it for the world. I don't know whether to polish my halo or sharpen my pitchfork!

10
The Peter-Paul Principle
(or Papa Pays & Pays & Pays)

"Money" is a dirty word. Dirty words were never allowed in my home. "Money" was no exception. Talk about money would be considered crass, uncouth, tacky. Wonder why? Is it sinful? Suspect? A substitute for love? Does it buy affection? Security? A mother substitute? A master? Used for power, love, manipulation, control, or success? A psychological fixation? We hear people say, "filthy rich," "stinking miser," "wallowing in money," and "the highest stakes are in the big pot."

The Good Book sets the record straight. Money is not the culprit. The *love* of it is (see 1 Tim. 6:10).

Money was no barometer, thermometer, scales, or rule of measurement in my home. Your smile was your barometer (see Prov. 3:17), your enthusiasm your thermometer (see Ps. 98:6), your fairness, your scales (see Prov. 11:1), and your rule the Golden Rule (see Matt. 7:12).

What a shock I was in for when I left the nest. I discovered money makes the world go round—a constant source of talk, speculation, and activity. It runs the gamut from admiration to worship. Festers envy, jealousy. Some wheel and deal, steal and kill for it; prevaricate, nauseate, and bellyache about it. That's nothing new. It's been that way since the beginning of time. The Good Book has lots to say about money. Ecclesiastes 7:12 is a defense, as is 10:19. Yet our

Lord was betrayed for thirty pieces of silver (see Matt. 26:15; 27:3,5-6,9).

I had no idea money would continue to play such a small part in my life. I should have gotten an inkling on my wedding day. After the reception, dressed in my "going-away" finery, I anticipated a semi-honeymoon. The trip from North Carolina to Georgia, where Chief was a senior in dental school, was my "honeymoon." It would require two long, exquisite days to make the trip in an old model car. We were to spend the first night twelve miles away in a hotel, the second night in South Carolina. His sister and her husband abandoned their apartment one night to accommodate the honeymooners.

I was ready. Chief was not. He took me to his parents' home, then disappeared. The bride on the sofa in the empty living room began having second thoughts. Those wedding tears! Had Chief changed his mind? Didn't he know about leaving your mama and papa? (see Eph. 5:31). Why the delay? The first Peter-Paul Principle: robbing Peter to pay Paul. He had to borrow from his Dad. Chief didn't have any money. Still doesn't. He's got ideas, ideals, dreams, goals, but no cash.

His first goal was to finish dental school. Goals shift. They are stepping stones. Success? Success is a matter of opinion—elusive, deceptive. A long friendship-turned-courtship allowed plenty of goal-setting for us. We knew we couldn't have both children and things (see Mark 10:23), and no stored-up treasures (see Luke 12:21). Children were our choice: our investments of time and money, our blessings—God willing. God loves children. He chose that way to bring His Son into the world (see Luke 1:31). He considers us His children (see John 3:50).

The Peter-Paul Principle continues. With this investment in children, we knew we could not do it alone. We have always needed, asked for, and received help from our Heavenly Father; Chief also looked for some earthly sources. He learned early the necessity of life insurance. He applied the Peter-Paul Principle of borrowing on the cash value, especially during college years. We managed to average three children in college at a time, five at the most. Chief looked to his insurance source to begin investing for the retirement years. Self-employed persons have no Big Daddies.

"Daddy, isn't it cheaper now?"

"What's cheaper, Son?"

"Raising a family. Don't buy as many tricycles, bikes."

"Trikes, bikes, and toys cost lots less than cars."

You see how much money was talked around Bedlam. Little ones didn't know. I wonder about the big ones. Thumbing, as in Chief's college days, was out. Instead of trading cars, Chief passed them down the line. We trusted their driving. It provided another work incentive.

Wheels were no problem for the young ones. That was Chief Santa's department. Santa could wander around on Christmas Eve and bargain hunt, invigorated by an earlier golf game. Most of the times he lucked into used trikes and bikes. Sometimes there was no time for paint jobs. One Christmas morning, one of our little bike riders came in puzzled.

"Daddy, that boy down the street said this was a used bike. Is this an old bike?"

"It's new to *you,* isn't it?"

"Yes, sir."

"Then it's a *new bike!*"

"Yes, sir," he grinned. Satisfied, he wheeled away.

Another letter to Santa requested an English bike, out of our financial reach that year.

"Dad, I asked Santa for an *English* bike! This is an *American* bike!"

"You can't fool Santa! He knows you're American. Why would you want an English bike? We're Americans. We pedal. Gives you stronger legs. With English bikes, gears and all, there's more to go wrong. They don't always work. Legs do. Be thankful you have legs that work!"

Work is another four-letter word. Our generation was not assaulted, insulted, embarrassed, intimidated by four-letter words. Ones allowed included *glad, live, pray, play,* and *work.* Work was rarely called a curse—but a privilege, tranquilizer, salvation. It was a verb meaning "action," a relative of the word *money.* No workee—No monee—No eatee. Work was a popular word. It was reality.

Just as my short stay in father's hotel oven prepared this "premy" for the future, so did Chief's childhood. We were Depression kids. Like Billy Graham, "We were poor but didn't know it." We thought we were rich. We had a roof over our heads, food on the table, warmth, friends, and family. Just no cash.

Sharing was a way of life. Never were the hungry or homeless turned away. Phrases like ". . . but for the grace of God . . . ," "If you do this unto the least of these . . ." and the Golden Rule were on every tongue tip. Parents had no worries about car accidents. We walked. It was less crowded. We learned it's never far to walk to a friend's house or float to a sweetheart's. Dates split five-cent drinks. Double dates shared packages of instant pudding—the newest thing around. Enjoyable evenings were spent cutting watermelons or turning a freezer of ice cream with friends. There was lots of small talk. Who's read what? Who's going steady? Who won the ball game? We bemoaned any friend who strayed from the straight and narrow. We had compassion for unavoidable school dropouts. World problems were left to adults to solve. We never thought we had that much sense. We thought wisdom came with age. There was a time and place for everything (Eccl. 3:1). Enjoy life now (Eccl. 2:24). Be content (see Phil. 4:11). Be thankful (see Eph. 5:20).

There were plays, concerts, and movies. Some could afford paints or musical instruments. There was no television, some radio. Phonographs and records were a luxury, the piano a magnet. Pianists were most popular. Everyone contributed to the party, was a part of the entertainment. You could sing, recite, and provide lots of shared laughs, fun, and togetherness. We had little. What little we had, we learned to take care of. There were no possessions to worry about or keep up with. The greatest possessions were good health, a sense of humor, and a good reputation (see Eccl. 7:1). They were second only to family and friends. The greatest watering holes were home, school, and church—our strength. We just didn't know any other way. Maybe much happiness is overlooked because it doesn't cost anything.

Grounded in history, we were well aware of our heritage. Work was a way of life. Chief was working when I first laid eyes on him. He still is. Then, it was at a grocery store from 7 AM to midnight. Before NRA. He still frequents grocery stores. Most men avoid them. For Chief, it's like a homecoming. At the age of ten his first job was delivering prescriptions for the neighborhood drug store. They provided a bicycle. Chief didn't have one. It was an incentive.

Chief still believes in incentives. The children are required to earn their first semester's college tuition. They have to want to invest in their own future. If they showed they did, then he sent them the rest of the way. Spending money is earned; everyone has to learn to support their habits. Sometimes I think we are getting back to the olden days. Olden days were formerly known as "these trying times." I saw a sign recently that read, "We use an incentive plan. Work or get fired."

Parents sacrificed to educate their children. No one loaned

students money. They were considered bad risks. No government grants. No handouts. Work and save. Chief was a carpenter and stonemason's helper during the summers. In winters he worked up from a laundry routeman to fraternity house manager. The frat job provided room, board, and dues. Buying groceries and planning meals were good training for raising a big family.

There were some delays and hitches to completing Chief's education. He can identify with today's students—those on five-year plans or dropouts. Between his freshman and sophomore years at dental school, he couldn't make enough money for tuition. He tasted the failure feeling. In spite of hard work, there just wasn't enough. My second brother sold his car to lend Chief the funds he needed that year. The Peter-Paul Principle and Golden Rule were still at work. My brother preferred walking or riding the bus. I was in college and engaged; Chief was now my investment. My brother didn't want an old maid on his hands.

Chief's pockets contained well-worn Norman Vincent Peale pamphlets. His messages were our mainstay. I even had the thrill of hearing him preach at Marble Collegiate Church in New York. It was so crowded, I couldn't get a seat in the sanctuary. When I came up from the basement, Dr. Peale was still at the door greeting people. We read him and used his prayers (see Eph. 6:18).

As old goals were met, new goals were set. Finish dental school. Talks with elder physicians convinced Chief dentistry was for him. He could support a big family and provide a service, with more time for family life, and fewer life-and-death situations. Medical doctoring is not for wedding weepers.

Dentistry is a do-it-yourself affair. It's hard work. Dentists have the second-highest suicide rate nationally. Eventually hearing "I hate to go to the dentist" gets to you year after year. Dentists are special—crazy. They have to acquire a protective armor (see Eph. 6:11), and have a great sense of humor. They are fun to be with socially. It helps them to cushion the complaints. To help Chief take them less personally, I made two signs for his lab, his between-patients refuge. "Everyone brings happiness to this office. Some by coming. Some by going," and "I can stand anybody thirty minutes."

Some wives can help their husbands. I can't, not in the dental office. I tried. I lasted half a day. Instead of shooting the stream of water on the cavity to keep it cool, it traveled up the patient's nostril through her eyebrow to the top of her beehive hair-do, before I got it under control. Instead of cavity checking, I was palate checking. Did you know that no two are alike? They're full of interesting humps? Chief advised me to take my curiosity elsewhere. I'm allowed only to help with decorating chores. Not chairside.

It's strange how some people can always figure your income, but never your expenses. "Married to a rich dentist. No wonder you can afford that big family." Unlike myself, they can't multiply. Nine children and a wife! How about years spent in expensive schooling, office set-ups, salaries, and overhead? Some make money for things they don't want, to impress people they can't stand. Chief makes money to buy shoes. Thank God he can work and they have feet. We asked for it. We'll survive, with the dear Lord's help and our hard work—balancing the Peter-Paul Principle.

Balance is a household word. When the Good Book is replaced by the bank book, we're out of balance. Our financial balance still employs the Peter-Paul Principle. Guess it always will. Who could foresee the price of living escalating out of sight? The value of the dollar falling? In fact, if you want to teach your children the value of a dollar, you'd better hurry.

Dentistry is not a salaried profession. It's based on faith and prayer. Chief does the work in good faith. He prays they will pay. Money sometimes comes in trickles or in a steady ebb and flow. It's rarely a tidal wave. Our bill-paying is likewise. The dear Lord understands such matters. "Forgive our debts as we forgive our debtors" (see Matt. 6:12, RSV).

11
Advice to New Fathers
(or The Envy or Enemy of the Neighborhood)

My first thought is, *Don't do it.* Obviously you have when you find your wife knitting bootees, accumulating baby clothes instead of bathing suits, reading baby books instead of fashion magazines.

With some folks you shouldn't brag about having babies. I disagree. I say—boast. Your neighbor may be willing to have children, but not able. A man that tends to his homework never has these worries (see 1 Cor. 7). So brag. That's the thing to do (see Eph. 5:28).

Fatherhood proves lots of things—that you're still young, virile, and *capable of procreation* says the dictionary. You're the envy of the neighborhood. Your stock with the opposite sex goes up. You can't hide success. Not for nine months anyway.

During the long-to-your-wife incubation period, you can be a great help, as if you haven't been enough already. You can be a poor man's Dale Carnegie. For instances: When your little lady, no longer little, large with child, catches you eyeing a slender dame, be a quick thinker. Change her envious look with a tender admission.

"I was just thinking, dear, how much better *you* look. You *know* you are desirable. You have proof."

If your spouse needs cheering, pick out a passing female with horrible legs or some impossible-to-you feature.

"Look, honey, *your* condition is temporary." Or, "You look better pregnant than she does *not*."

Remember good businessmen look after their investments. This is one investment that is guaranteed to reap dividends if you show a little interest. You must have to have gotten these results.

Go along with her strange food cravings. Melons in January or country ham at midnight might be inconvenient but delicious. Put a little fun in your life—eat strange food at strange times. That gives you something to talk about.

When you catch your wife glancing sideways in a full-length mirror, be quick to say, "These matching outfits are neat. Not only pretty but sensible. Wish they'd dream up something comfortable for men. Guess leisure suits were the nearest thing."

Take a good look at yourself in the mirror. Check your middle, remarking, "Could use one myself. I look a little pregnant."

You can make those nine months memorable. Together rediscover the beauties of nature as you squire her proudly around the block for a nightly constitutional. Be protective. Don't let her stumble. Not only a point builder, you'll be the envy of the neighborhood, or enemy, according to who's looking out the windows. A brisk walk will make you both sleep well. New father, get your sleep. It becomes a rare commodity in the fullness of time!

When you get that middle-of-the-night nudge, when you hear that long-awaited declaration, "Darling, this is it!"—don't panic! Don't wonder why it is always in the middle of night, just like you heard. There's no time to ponder. Count to nine. Ten might be too late. Calmly ask, "Honey, are you sure? Have you checked the clock? The book?"

If she doesn't throw it at you, be firm. Be in command. Remind her of false labor. She doesn't want to make a trip back home unrewarded. Mothers-to-be hate losing face worse than their shapes. Pretend to go back to sleep. She won't. Her eyes will be glued to the clock.

Who do you think you're fooling? Pretending to know all about everything. You remember the chapter, "How to Deliver Babies at Home"? Visions of gallons of hot water. Where are the clippers? How about scissors? Knives? That's enough to make you sit up in bed. Thinking of your own hands cutting the cord will get you into your clothes, entreating, "Let's go, honey! On the double!"

At the slightest protest, ". . . but *you* said."

"Never mind what *I* said! You might be different!"

Don't bother to shave. No one looks at the father anyway. It's dangerous to shave. You might cut yourself. There's no demand for cutthroat fathers. They just want you to pay the bill. Hope you wrote down your name, your father's name, your mother's name. Do you know your wife's maiden name? They can ask the most irritating questions sometimes!

If you are of the old school, give the imminently new mother a "good-luck-I-love-you" kiss. Leave as quickly as possible. Don't look back. Your job is done. You started this production. She has to finish it herself. No husband, father, mother, doctor, or friend can do it for her. There's no time for nonsense, no quips like, "Don't worry, dear. Everything will come out all right in the end," or "Everything's coming up rosy," or "You're way out in front!" Rarely do first moms have a sense of humor. It is not time to test it. Remember there is a time for everything. This is not the time for your Bozo role.

If you are lucky enough to have fathering classes in your town, you won't be cheated. You'll know how Adam felt. When you first see your own flesh and blood, your child, you'll know firsthand how much our Heavenly Father loves us (see John 3:16). You still have a choice. To stay or go. Don't be intimidated or coerced into participating or not. That's between you and your wife. Your behavior will fool no one, most especially your wife. You don't even have to walk the floor. The baby will come whether or not you are ready. The Good Lord's with her (see Matt. 28:20). The promise is yours. Claim it.

There's nothing more useless than a walk-the-floor father. This rat-in-a-maze activity does appeal to some martyr complexes; if you have one, pamper it. Some men take to the nearest coffee shop to sip black java. You can tell the oldtimers. They go home, either to look after the little ones or crawl into their sacks. They know about precious sleep.

Sleep or not, the telephone ring ends speculation. Boy or girl? If bedside, you'll learn about love at first sight. Boy or girl won't register. "How's my wife?" is about all you can croak. They'll lead you to the source of all your worries and pleasure in due time. You'll discover she's probably in better shape than you. Women are built for these things, you know (see Luke 1:42). Thank God!

Alone with your love, forgetting to be your usual funny man self, you ask, in all seriousness, "How did it go, dear?"

"A jazzed-up version of 'From Here to Maternity,' " she smiles.

Take your cue.

"Maybe for you. But for me it was a warmed-over version of, 'From here, it's eternity!' "

Between tears and kisses you'll hear how the littlest angel favors you. If you're lucky, you'll get to see him or her. Once home, you'll dream of that picture of perfection, your newborn. The thrill of fatherhood has no equal (see 1 Tim. 6:17).

The first month at home with your new family could be likened to your army hitch—something you have to go through with. No routine is foolproof. Babies can't be filed, computed, or fathomed. They are half mouth and half plumbing. Admittedly there are times we think we can feed the world. We are blessed with short memories. The bottle-and-diaper routine is soon forgotten. New mothers? What about them?

You've heard about labor. Now a word about management. Fathers, never is it more important than now for role learning. You learned to make a living. You took coaching in your sport's pursuits. What about father preparation? Did you know you are part of a divine order? You are the priest, king, and prophet of your home. God intends it that way (see 1 Cor. 13:4-6).

Goethe said, "Women are to be loved, not understood." I made Chief a sign for his bedside, to jog his memory. Proverbs 10:1,15,20 tell us that a wise man makes a glad father. This head-of-the-household role is Scriptural (see 1 Cor. 11:3). You don't learn it overnight. Marriage and/or fatherhood doesn't bring instant success, like a television drama to be solved in thirty minutes. Like maturity, it takes time, prayerful reflection, study, and action (see Eph. 6:1,4).

There is plenty of action in fatherhood. Suddenly our world changes. We are not just ourselves. We're just not the cutest couple in our crowd. We're a family, a unit, a part of the natural unfolding of God's plan for us. With the blessing of children, it is time to take stock. Time for prayerful study and reflection.

Why marriage? God didn't intend for us to live alone. (see Eccl. 9:9). He has someone just right for us picked out (see Gen. 2:18). It isn't always the one of our choice. I know. Chief was my friend—fun. Marriage material? Never! He had all the things that count—good character, fine morals. His disposition, temperment, and dependability were circumspect in my book. But he was immature. If he ever grew up, I thought he'd be a super husband. I didn't think I could wait that long.

I didn't consider what a raw deal he'd be getting. I, too, was immature. I wanted a soft-spoken "head of the house." Chief was a free spirit. He liked to soar. So did I. I thought it would be disastrous to have two in a family. I thought he was a surface person, not caring about delving into the bottom of anything.

God has shown me how wrong I was (see Jas. 5:16, 1 Cor. 13:5). I thought I couldn't live with him. There's no way I could live without him. I knew I couldn't change him. I've never entertained thoughts of changing anyone, especially my husband. The only time you can change a man is when he's in diapers. I had had plenty of that by the time I said "I do." I tried and am still trying to be the best possible wife—pleasing to God (see Prov. 3:4-6; 17:22); to be true to myself; to be able to weather whatever; to try to bring out the best in my husband, to be his greatest asset (see Eccl. 9:9).

Chief and I not only need each other (see 1 Cor. 11:11-12), we deserve each other (see 1 Cor. 11:3). There is no doubt I have been playing my God-given role of "responder" (see Gal. 6:7). I know I want to be ruled (see Gen. 3:16).

Priority straightening isn't an overnight accomplishment. It is a lifelong adventure. There have been times when I thought I was low down on Chief's totem pole, and times when I made great strides. I even came from seventh to fifth in one year! Other times I stayed at a standstill (see Heb. 12:15). It took maturing on my part to realize I was pleasing the wrong one (see Eph. 6:10-11).

Chief was not pleasing me on one of my nights out. I was anticipating a party. We had out-of-town guests. Chief slipped in and out of the room. About time I was ready to introduce our friends, he wasn't around. I had the whole host's role. *He* had invited them. Exasperating! I would spy Chief turning down lights, then talking with someone else.

"Chief was president of the club *last year,*" I explained to our guests. "Probably enjoyed it so much, he can't quit."

"Libbylove, I found out who's president of this club. You recall we couldn't remember?" A friend remarked.

"Would you believe—Chief?"

"No wonder he's so busy!" I hastened to apologize for my bad-mouthing.

When Chief returned to our table, I apologized to him for what I thought was bad manners, bordering neglect.

"I just found out you're president of this club. How many other clubs are you president of?"

"Would you believe three?" He enumerated them. "Just lucky, they all came up at the same time."

"When are you going to be president of our outfit?—your family?" I teased.

When you love your wife, you are loving yourself (see Eph. 5:28). We can't begin to love God, until we love ourselves (see Matt. 22:37-39).

12
Open Wide
(or I Practice Medicine Without a License)

"Open wide" is Chief's line. It's a good dental diagnostic tool. Bumps, ulcers, and bleeding gums are a sure sign something's amiss. This body barometer wasn't an overnight discovery with me. It took years of home medical practice to acquire, in my home, with my children.

Children #1 and 2 were born on an army post. Trips to the base hospital pediatrician completely confused me as to "proper baby care." No wonder they call army wives and children "dependents."

One week later Capt. Jones saw my offspring.

"What are you giving them?" he asked.

"What do you mean?" I timidly inquired.

"No vitamins?" he boomed.

"No, no vitamins. Lots of orange juice, cod-liver oil, and fresh air," I said apologetically.

"How cruel!" He glared. "Throw away that old-fashioned stuff! Give them vitamins X, Y, and Z!"

Crushed, I slipped into the nearest pharmacy and loaded up. Broke but smug, I took the children for their next scheduled checkup.

"Capt. Jones has been transferred. Lt. Smith will see them today," I was told.

Lt. Smith inspected the children thoroughly, clicked his teeth, and cleared his throat.

"What are you giving the children?"

I was prepared this time.

"Vitamins X, Y, and Z," I happily replied.

"Greatest waste of time and money known to man!" He gave me a disgusted look. "Just feed them well-balanced meals. Save your poor husband's money."

These sessions convinced this dependent to become independent. There are as many different schools of thought in the medical field as there are specialties—plenty.

Prayerfully, I thought about my autonomy, my responsibility for my life, my right to trial and error, my refusal to conform. I realized my parental responsibility. My children were an outgrowth of my own autonomy. Philosophy. I reread my hang-in-there theory (see Eph. 6:10), patience in afflictions (see Jas. 5), especially prayerfully handling sickness (James 5:13).

My childhood painted my philosophical picture. There had been no medicine cabinet. My mom was a practicing faith healer. Prayer had gotten through. I often felt neglected. Tiny pink calomel pills or sulphur and molasses were never a springtime ritual as in other Southern households. After my incubator beginning and medicine dropper feedings, I was a healthy child.

If my friends complained of a stomachache, they kept it to themselves. The sight of thick, colorless castor oil prompted many an instant recovery. Castor oil's been around since biblical times. The plant afforded the prophet Jonah shade. The seeds contained the oil. Although in high repute as a medicine for ages, it was never used in my house. My mom plied us with raisins and figs.

I never ran to mama unless mortally wounded. You knew she would douse hurts with liquid fire—iodine. I never wore bandages like battle ribbons. Thought it best to let the air cure the wound—to let it breath. A scratch? A hug was the remedy. My Mom thought it took hugs to survive. I stayed aboard the playship if I could navigate at all. A trip ashore to mama surely meant being quarantined to sick bay. I didn't want that. Living in a hotel, if I had something contagious, I was shipped off to a hospital.

Sickness at home didn't mean radio, television, colorful medicine, and flavorful pills. With luck I found a pencil, paper, and crayons. Books were my salvation. If someone caught a youngster lying under a tree, alone, eyes contemplating the heavens, it was not earthshaking. No cause for parental alarm. Dreaming dreams was understandable. No dreamers were considered likely candidates for psychiatric treatment.

Torn between olden-days medicine and vacillating army advice, I collected my own medical ammunition—the Bible, my mom's preventive medical methods, U.S. Government pamphlets galore, Milton Senn's *All About Feeding Children,* and Emily Post's *Children Are People.* Dr. Spock's book was a best-seller. One perusal convinced me we were worlds apart philosophically. The chapter on when to call the doctor was helpful. Government pamphlets were concise, clear, and free. *Parents* magazine replaced *Vogue.* So equipped, I started practicing medicine on my brood without a license.

I didn't have a license for juggling. The jesting juggler was my role. I struggled to find the right balance between care and neglect, trying not to seem so concerned I would spawn unnecessary anxiety. I tried not to cripple my children emotionally by imprisoning them to me by planting doubts of their own self-sufficiency.

Yearly checkups were a must. Bumps, scratches, and bruises were hugged and kissed away. Tummy aches and constipation were analyzed and treated. Low-grade fevers, sore throats, and colds were under a watchful eye with plenty of hugs and "no big deal" comments.

Thoughtfully, prayerfully, I made my own judgments. No more battles of sleep with open windows vs. night air is harmful; spanking vs. ignore the crime; wash hair of child with bad cold vs. dirty hair causes cradle cap. They all had required immunizations. Unless they ran high temperatures, I doctored them. Hug therapy was prevalent.

Prevalent germs among my nine forced me into a group practice. Children #1 through #4 were bedded down with mumps. My contracting them complicated matters. It didn't help to learn my maid couldn't read. It did account for the brine she called soup. She didn't know to add water to the can. It was not her fault 'cause she was new on the job. We had just moved into Trinity Treat and were completely surrounded by packing boxes. Boxes can wait but not sick children.

To make matters worse, we were all set for a trip to Florida to see my mom. The healthy children enjoyed being alive. They flaunted their good fortune all through the house. They cried out against the injustice of having to miss a trip to grandmother's house. Chief was understandably noncommittal. My pediatrician solved the mumps madness by letting us go to Florida—mumps and all. There was happiness all around. This sage doctor, a partner in my practice, said, "Four have it. More can get it just as well in Florida as North Carolina. You know what to do."

I didn't know what to do about the chicken-pox caper. It got a little testy. This doc soon tired of running from bed to bed. Each child wanted to be read to and played with. Chicken pox is chicken pox. So the four miserable minors were plunked into one bed, two on each side. There I sympathized and entertained at one fell swoop. Being most careful that the banished well babies were not envious, moans were forthcoming each time they appeared at the doorway. "Off limits" signs were plastered around.

"Off limits" were hated, especially if you were the only one in sick bay. They thought they were abandoned. The brother or sister they were on good terms with snuck the patient some contraband. The exposed child soon contracted the ailment. The truth became known.

I like a group practice better than a single one. Measles lasted for months with one at a time. It seemed a never-ending battle. This doc struggled to keep nine pairs of hands washed a minimum of three times a day. Masks were part of the modus operandi.

Some of the masks were strange. A mixture of Dr. Kildare, Halloween, and Mardi Gras. Especially the mask child #4—son #3—wore when he had poison ivy. I hated poison ivy. I doctored so much of it, the children endured the ailment far longer than they should. They suffered in silence until the rash was unbearable. I was the plant hunter. Tried to ferret out the pest from our yard. I adore woods. I made sure we built our house in them. It served me right. Ticks and poison ivy required daily checks.

Once I took a violent case of poison ivy to the physician. He prescribed gentian violet tablets in soaking water. Having an almost white tub, in spite of unscheduled naval battles, I balked. I did not want to change my color scheme to purple. We compromised. I used gentian violet, but mixed the solution in a huge tin tub. Child #4—son #3—took one look at the old-fashioned tub. He balked. I pointed out the tubs on television westerns. I even provided a cowboy hat. I dragged the tub full of liquid medication to the woods back of the house, and I marched the reluctant poison ivy victim to the secluded spot. Only when I produced an old Halloween mask to cover his face, would he cooperate. Assured no one would recognize him, he soaked away. He spent a nervous hour wondering who was behind the trees. Years later, the truth came out. His brothers sold tickets in the neighborhood—to an exclusive few, of course, to see the "purple people eater."

Thank goodness dermatologists have come up with better poison ivy remedies! My group practice flourished once with four boys covered with the itchy rash. I put two in each twin bed and set my compressing equipment between the beds. I compressed two on one side while the other two entertained us with song. I switched to the other two. They tired of the whole routine before I did. Luckily for me the song, "Poison Ivy", was popular. I bought a copy of it. They didn't think it was funny. I didn't think the whole drippy mess was funny, either. I tried and failed.

"Mom, you compressed him twice and forgot all about me!"

That did it. I gathered up the powders and lotions and marched into the bathroom. I calculated how many gallons of water would fill the tub. I dropped in the correct amount of the medication, stirring it with a baseball bat. I doused the four poison-ivy kids in the tub. They were happier with this setup. I left them soaking.

I went downstairs for a cup of coffee and an attitude adjustment. I looked up at my sign, "I can do all things through Christ who strengthens me." I sent up prayer patter. Soon I was ready for magazines. Couldn't decide which to read—the article, "Would you Marry the Same Man?" or "The Changing Status of Women." No problem. The answer came from upstairs. The soaking had become a swimming party. I sped to the happy splashers who now had goose bumps, blue mouths, and shriveled skin—but they were medicated.

When illness struck, I made rounds with bed check and a chart. I had a paper plate with the patient's name on it. I put the medication and directions on the plate, thus assuring the right child received the right medicine for the right ailment on the right time. Like hospitals, I also goof. I discovered earache oil opens up nasal passages pronto. The bottles were so similar in shape. It made me more alert, made me call on the Great Physician even more.

With any practicing physician, there's never a dull moment. Just when you think your practice has calmed down, the weather will change, and a child will start sniffling.

"Mom, I'm taking cold. What am I gonna do?"

Flattered he would consider my medical advice, I cooed in my best bedside manner, "Plenty of rest, aspirin, and orange juice."

He nodded solemnly. I resumed my housework, gloating over my sensible child. Glancing out the window, I saw my young patient in short sleeves, playing a bruising game of touch football. Like other physicians, I wonder how you can practice good medicine when your patients refuse to do what you tell them.

Medical miseries tested me. Child #2—son #1—was literally climbing the wall with pain and was hospitalized. I couldn't believe those in authority expected me to leave him. A tap on the shoulder. An order to leave. Visiting hours were over.

"Can't treat children as easily with parents around."

"I can't leave him. What will he think? Abandon him in his great pain? Never. He'd never forgive me—or forget."

All my cries were met with firmness. Out I went. Orders. Crying all the way home didn't help. Tons of prayers pulled me through. Thank God most hospitals have changed their policies. They are now more child-considerate than medically convenient.

An infected lymph node was the culprit. A red appendix was removed. When he was put in isolation for suspected polio a few years later, I still wasn't allowed in the room. There were spinal taps. Only the dear Lord's strong arm upholds you through such a crisis. Everything that went into the room was burned sterile. So joyfully thankful there was no permanent damage to my son, memories of wailing and gnashing of teeth vanished.

Memories of the polio scare remain. No children were allowed to attend public gatherings of any kind. We were cautioned to keep calm and cool, and afternoons were spent trying to keep them still. They were required to lie down. Books, games, and puzzles were shared under the trees where there was shade and an occasional breeze. No sun was allowed. We gathered strength from one another. My source never failed (see Luke 22:32). The children sensed a crisis and were cooperative.

Everyone reacts differently to a crisis. Child #3—son #2—was riding double on a bike with a friend. They wheeled out into the street to avoid a dog snapping at their britches. They headed toward the next driveway. An automobile hit them. Child #3—son #2's—head was three inches from the tire. The car ran over his leg and broke it in two places. I didn't see or hear it. I heard an ambulance—nothing unusual. Those vehicles often zoomed up and down the busy street in front of Trinity Treat.

The knock on the door brought the bad news. My maid started moaning, "What we gonna' do?"

"Start praying. Look after the little ones until I get back from the hospital."

"How can you be so calm?"

"Because I have to be."

#1 child—#1 daughter—popped up from behind the back seat of the car as I pulled away from the house.

"You shouldn't have come," I said, "You know they don't allow children in hospitals as visitors."

"I'll wait in the car, Mom. I always go with you when the little ones get hurt. You need me."

How right she was! This self-appointed worrier could offer more comfort with her big blue eyes (see Ps. 107:28-29).

Chief was a different matter. He had weathered the polio crisis calmly. He only missed a golf game while #2 child—#1 son—was hospitalized. That was a sure sign of anxiety.

After comforting and reassuring the auto-bike collision casualty, I flew to Chief's office. He didn't know about it.

"Aren't we two of the luckiest . . ."

"What in the world was he doing riding double in the street? Stupid!"

Acid in the face! Knife-in-the-back feelings! I tucked my hurts inside. Then I went by the office where the other mother worked. Her son didn't have a scratch. We exchanged hugs of thankfulness. After sending up plenty of "Thanks, Lord," I went home to reassure the other children. Number 1 child was still by my side.

Busy at home, spending every spare minute with the hospitalized one, I was numb. The hurt was compounded by Chief's actions. He wasn't speaking to me at all. Two weeks seemed like two years. I couldn't seem to hear what my Heavenly Father was saying to me. There was no one else to share my hurts and fears with. I decided to tell Chief's mother.

Trembling, apologizing and, scared, I slipped over to my in-laws. Words tripped over one another as I painfully reviewed the past two weeks. Child #3—son #2's—leg didn't hurt, even after resetting, like his feelings. Guilt had caused the cystitis, according to his urologist who suggested I find a cot and stay with my little son. It was cheaper than a round-the-clock-nurse. No longer was I abandoning a child in his hour of need. The only spur in my saddle was Chief. Younger children were taken care of. Not speaking was punishment—torture!

Chief's parents were home, thank God, to hear my tale of woe. They hugged me with their eyes, if not their arms. They had the supreme suggestion. "Let's pray about it!"

Down on our knees we plopped. Silently we prayed, no words, no hugs. A learning experience for me. I learned words aren't necessary. Neither are hugs. Just prayers. I felt my first everlasting bond with them. I learned we all react differently to crisis, and I also learned to thank God for the bad as well as the good. I felt closer to my husband's family. "And we know that all things work together for good to them that love God" (see Rom. 8:28). I discovered I was wise to limit my practice of medicine to children. Mine. I couldn't do much for adults—especially me.

13
Libbylove vs. Television
(or I Want to Be Front and Center)

"Has anyone in our family ever been in jail?"

I almost dropped the heavy casserole I was carrying. Maybe I was hearing things. Maybe the television.

"Hey, Libbylove. Mom, has anyone in our family . . . ?"

I rushed into the living room of our Psychiatric Saltbox home. Child #2—Son #1—didn't have a chance to finish his question.

"*Of course not!*" I dammed up my flow of ready words when I saw him. Mesmerized he watched the jail door clank shut. He was so engrossed in television, he never looked up. I did. Heavenward. Sending up one more, "Be calm. Think. Don't over-react." I knew I had to make my peace with television sooner or later. I had to face it. "The thing which I greatly feared is come upon me . . . and that which I was afraid of is come unto me" (see Job 3:25).

"Tell me, Mom, has anyone in the family ever been in jail?"

"Probably should have been," I laughed. "But not to *my* knowledge. Besides, there are lots of *kinds* of jails."

He was in no mood for the Jesting Juggler. He was serious.

"Finish your program, son. We'll talk about jails during supper chores."

He went back to his dream world. I struggled with this

one. High time I tell them who they are, where they came from, what kind of folks their ancestors were. I mustn't tell too much, or too little. Where else could they get this knowledge? Osmosis? These were rather heavy questions, even for me. I was supposed to be wiser and was sho 'nuff older.

During supper chores children #1 and 2 were told who they were one more time—God's children. He made us (see Eph. 1:4). He loaned them to us. Life is also a gift to be enjoyed. After several I-know-thats, "tell me about jails" persisted. I made several attempts at the short version. Your ancestors were preachers, teachers, physicians, lawyers, and missionaries. Service to humanity was their theme song. No. They wanted the long version. Especially pleas of, "Didn't any of them ever get in trouble?"

"Briefly. One kinsman fought a duel over a parcel of land. It was the custom then. Just like you see on TV."

They whistled appreciatively.

"What happened? Did he get in jail?"

"No jail. They both were killed. Let me tell you about my missionary cousin," I hastened to change the subject.

"Don't want to hear about that. Dull!"

"China wasn't dull. Did you know they used to bind up little girls' feet?" I knew that would appeal to the girl-haters. A flicker of interest surfaced. "Those they didn't want, they threw in the brink." Eyes bulged. "Cousin Venetia pulled many a one out. She even adopted a Chinese boy. Educated him here in the States." Thought I had their attention.

"Okay, but didn't anyone do anything interesting?"

"Designed and made playground equipment for Coney Island."

"*Jails,* Mom!"

"Sorry to disappoint you. The nearest thing was that my

maternal granddaddy was run out of town. He was a lawyer and his office was ransacked."

"Why?"

"Civil War days. He believed slaves should be freed. Because of that he suffered great torment and hardship. It's not easy to stand for what you believe, especially when brothers, family, friends, and neighbors don't agree."

Now I was front and center.

"That grandfather wasn't the first relative to feel that way about slavery. My revolutionary paternal grandfather freed his slaves. He understood oppression for he was a French Huguenot. He was run out of France for his religious beliefs. He went from Ireland to England to Virginia. There's a Methodist Church he built still standing. It's important to take a stand and stick by it. That's like the sign over there, "If you don't stand up for something, you'll fall for anything."

They were hooked. I warmed to my subject.

"Not just my family. America was founded by hardworking, God-fearing folks. Christopher Columbus thought his ministry was to take The Word to the 'second part of the world.' The first land he sighted, he named San Salvador after our Savior. When they couldn't agree on writing the Constitution, everyone thinking of their own interests, it was Ben Franklin who said, 'Stop, let us pray.' Congress has started with a prayer ever since. Ben Franklin prayed for our country then. We need to pray for it now. Prayer keeps us free."

We discussed freedom and bondage. I told them most of the latter is of our own making: our habits, our addictions, our choices. Again the Juggling Jester warmed to a captive audience.

"We can't choose our ancestors, and we can't rest on their laurels. We can't help their faults, but we can uphold their standards. We have that choice (see Gal. 6:3). We are ourselves—unique. We don't own each other but we belong to God (see 1 John 5:19). He gives us a mind (see Phil. 4:7) so we can choose. We can go through the supermarket of life, sampling. It's dumb to choose something harmful and poisonous. There is nothing new under the sun (see Eccl. 1:9). Temptation has been around a long time (see Gen. 22:1). The Good Book calls us to be moderate in all things (see Phil. 4:5), to have balance in our lives (see Prov. 11:1) to have guideposts. Will we choose a dreamworld or the real world? (see Rom. 13:11)

Television unlimited is a dreamworld—the secondhand living of spectators. John 10:10 tells us about the promised abundant life. We don't want to miss it, don't want our children to miss it. How can we learn to enjoy this life? (see 1 Cor. 2:9). By developing our awareness, by keeping our childlike delight in God's creation (see Matt. 18:3), by developing our capacity to live fully (see Rom. 6:11-13). A stay in the dreamworld nixes our chances for developing our senses (see Eccl. 11:4), and causes us to miss many astonishing things (see Isa. 55:3).

You do astonishing things, especially front and center. You can think up alternatives to television. It's not done in a judgmental way (see Rom. 14:13). Just throw out bait. "Let's put on our own TV show." You have only ten short years, if you're lucky, to be director, producer, and financial backer of your own home theatre. Take advantage. Remember, the first two years of your baby's life doesn't need all that television stimulation. Violence, unsavory characters, lewd acts will creep into your home soon enough via television. As long as you can keep the troops in line, don't desert them. Keep your ammunition handy (see Acts 17:28; 1 Cor. 2:9; Eccl. 12:13-14). Take charge (see Eccl. 12:11). There are alternatives.

Alternatives to television include a sampling of music, drama, sports, recitations, debates, or a combination of them all. It can be a showcase for what they have learned, a reward for all that carpooling to lessons, music, ballet ad nauseum. Some took, some didn't. I suffered no loss of sleep over the results. I just wanted to be sure they were exposed to good influences. Each child had opportunities to discover or develop his or her God-given talents (see Luke 19:11-28). Each success, however small, gives a feeling of confidence. Christmas plays were the most rewarding, the most enjoyed. Most would dive right in, loving every minute of the production. Others required reverse psychology. At least it made a more appreciative adult audience.

Confessing my monumental failures, I attempted to identify with the kids, and hoped and prayed they could identify with me (see Heb. 5:2; 1 Pet. 3:8). Reverse psychology and true confession trapped me. Now they say, "Good grief, Mom, why do I have to be like you? I'm no good at that! I can't do it!"

"*Can't* is a word that's not allowed!"

Try is the name of the game. Exercise, physical fitness, participation in sports are also great alternatives to TV. *Play* is an acceptable four-letter word in our household. It's at the top of Chief's totem pole. Nothing interferes with his play time. Birthdays, weddings, funerals and meetings are arranged around this important, necessary part of his life. It's necessary for his health, his disposition, his attitude, his balance.

"Children not idle and trouble-prone if involved in sports," Chief expounds when front and center—"It's an opportunity for togetherness."

Chief likes togetherness best of all. Sports give him time with friends. He participates in tennis and golf now. Gone are the basketball, softball, volleyball, and football—aged-out. Lest you think Chief's a "super jock," hear the story he tells on himself. In junior high school his coach suggested he take up wrestling. He was too small for football—might have gotten hurt. My oldest brother was the wrestling coach. Time will tell about hurts. Our school newspaper told this news bit:

> "What blonde boy works out with the wrestling squad days and with the coach's sister nights?"

Do I know a full nelson from a half nelson? My wrestling prowess came in handy with boyfriends, swains, Chief, and seven braves. No hammerlocks were used.

Chief learned to handle his 135 pounds well enough to play blocking back on our state championship football team. It was his confidence-builder. This led to public-speaking development. He had to talk about the football team before the student body. His football coach called each player aside before the championship game for a scouting report and pep talk. He individually told them how to play better and win. Chief, the smallest squad member, was first-string blocking back. The coach told him there was only one blocker in the whole state better than he. That gave Chief confidence, boosting him to do his best—made him think he could do the job.

After they won the state championship, Chief reminded the coach about his scouting report.

"You said there's only one blocker in the state better than I am, Coach. Who is the fellow?"

His teammates listened eagerly.

"Any big man!" the coach laughingly admitted.

Our Heavenly Coach spared Chief's life twice in World War II. Sports played a part. A regular participant in Ping-Pong, tennis, softball, and basketball at the Air Corps post, Chief carried on his own sports program. In addition to regular contests, one of his superiors loved to schedule extra games with Chief. He loved to play tennis and Ping-Pong with him. Somehow Chief always won—except once. Chief's promotion was due and hadn't come through. There were two little mouths to feed, plus my big one. He lost his tennis match to his superior officer. This equally sports-loving and competitive guy vowed to keep Chief on base until he beat Chief again.

Chief was due to ship out with a company of combat engineers. They needed a dentist, so his superior found another one. We didn't know it. Another time orders came. And down came the curtains and pictures. Then another phone call arrived from another superior, "You can't take *my* dentist!" In both instances we learned the ships were bombed in the Mediterranean Sea. The dentists went down with their crew (see 1 Sam. 22:23). Chief dwelt in safety (see Prov. 27:1).

Chief's pastimes (and ours) and occupation have saved his (and our) necks through the years—but the Good Lord planned it all. Praise His Name.

14
It's Questionable
(or Children Grow on You)

"Mom, how do you decline . . .?" The kitchen sounds drowned out the words. I turned three chickens over in the pan, covered the sizzling noise, and turned off the exhaust fan. I gave my eldest my undivided attention.

"You may write a note, telephone, or decline in person, Take your choice. All are correct."

"Mom! This is *Latin!* Don't you remember declining nouns, pronouns, adjectives? *Latin,* Mom!"

"Sorry. Thought you meant a social invitation," I called after her retreating figure.

"What's ailing her?" #2 child—#1 son—asked, coming into the kitchen, snitching chicken livers from under the lid.

"Questions! Questions! That's all I hear." I kept on cooking. "I have a question. Who has what this week?"

Number 2 child—#1 son—checked the work chart. It was so large it filled the poster board with one week's chores. Children's names were listed down the left-hand side according to age. The next column was the duty roster. The last column contained detailed job descriptions.

The chore chart was a rule, anchor, reality—the scene of much bargaining, a practice ground for neophyte diplomats and con artists.

"I have supper," #2 child scanned the work chart. "Number 1 has children. Number 3 has breakfast. Numbers 4 and 5 have dishes. Number 6 has table setting."

The supper hour. What fun to admire my offspring, the table setter. It's a time to check their growth, an opportunity to chat, Not to mention having a helping hand, the supper assistant. This one learned to cook—one recipe at a time.

"I'll toss the salad," #2 child—#1 son—offered, "I love to do that." He got out his favorite ingredients. "Hope #1 daughter remembers #7 child—#2 daughter—lost a tooth. She forgot to put money under her pillow last time."

"I heard complaints," I confided. "Number 7 said the tooth fairy must be a male."

"She has a thing about boys. She has five older brothers and two younger! She wanted to know what happened to the teeth the fairies collected. Did they get those from Chief's office?"

Lids clanked as child #5—son #4—checked supper fare.

"Chicken again? Where's that leftover roast? I was hoping you would make a Chinese dish out of it." He shared my love of cooking. When left to babysit the young ones, he would open my cookbooks and do his thing. Good cakes.

"Roast? Number 6 child—#5 son—used it last night," my inquisitor bounced around me.

"What would a four-year-old need a roast for?"

"I told him to get the dog out," I explained, playing dodge and taking up supper. "Spot wouldn't budge. Chief suggested a piece of food as bait. Spot took the suggestion! It was no trouble getting him outside."

"Not the roast?" #5 son hollered, springing higher.

"Sure did!" I put my elbows out to guard the food I was carrying. "Not a wiener or cold cut like Chief expected. Roast!"

"I know bananas never make it to pudding or nuts to

cakes but *roast* before Chow Mein!" Number 5 danced alongside me.

"Get lost," #2 child—#1 son—interrupted. "This is my time with Mom. How can the table setter ever make it with you weaving back and forth?"

The table setter and roast runner were one and the same. He was so intent on his new job, he was oblivious to the kitchen chatter.

"Do I have everything, Mom? Check me."

Could this be the same boy we cajoled, begged, and bribed into working last year? A 365-day miracle! His pale blue eyes sparkled with pride. His newest accomplishment—table setting.

"Looks great, Son." I kissed the top of his head. His 'branches,' as he calls his stubby hair, tickled my nose. "You remembered salt and pepper."

"Great?" #4 child—#3 son—came in the dining room. "Why so many spoons?"

"Say something nice or nothing!" I admonished. I absentmindedly patted #3 child—#2 son's—shoulder blades. His posture improved momentarily. He slumped into his seat at the table. *He hasn't held himself the same since his accident,* I worried.

"Bet I did bettern' that when I was young," #5 commented. This old man of eight years slid into his place.

"This is not the complaint department or battleground." I hugged the tiny table setter whose eyes were misting. "This is his *first* year on the work chart. There was a first for each of you."

I hugged with one arm. I caught the arm of a leaper (not leper) with the other, scolding, "You know the difference in outdoor behavior and indoor behavior! Basketball's an outdoor game around here. Those door facings won't survive."

"I'm getting taller," #4 child—#3 son—grinned. "I

couldn't touch the ceiling last year!" He planted a forgive-me kiss before strutting to his seat, also throwing an imaginary basket before sitting down.

"Do other houses have fingerprints on the ceilings?" I asked, dipping up the food. I served the plates, formally. I couldn't stand to see food spilling out of serving bowls as little hands attempted to pass them. "I'm so short I never noticed ceilings."

"Do you notice walls?" #1 child—#1 daughter—glared at her little sister. "You can't miss the Magic Marker, Mom!"

The cherubic culprit lowered her head. Not before sending a worshipful look towards her older sister.

"She *can* make an A!" I announced. "Look at it that way."

"Has had lots of practice," one boy whispered, amid laughs.

"Somebody . . ." I looked around the big table, ". . . somebody wrote that little girl's name on the upstairs hall wall. She is smart but can't write her name yet." All eyes were on their plates.

"What's going on?" Chief stood at the dining room door. "Let me guess. A convention of midgets? Indoor picnic for elves?"

"Daddy, Daddy, Daddy!" The two youngest boys fluttered around him. The little girl hugged him around the knees. "Hail to the Chief!" the rest chorused.

"No picnic," I smiled, "just hungry wolves, eating and growling."

"We're your children, Daddy!" #8 informed him.

"Chicken again?" Chief looked heavenward. "Fried this week. Last week, tetrazini. Next week, cacciatore. Every way but Russian."

"I wouldn't eat it!" #5 child—#4 son—declared.

"Russians are good cooks," Chief said. "You like chicken Kiev."

"Good soldiers," #4 child—#3 son—added.

"So good we need fallout shelters," #3 child—#2 son—declared.

"Who says?" Chief asked.

"We have papers for you to sign," #1 son—said.

"Me, too. Me, too." The older ones chorused.

"What kind of papers? I get writer's cramp easily."

"What you want us to do in case of an attack?" #1 child—explained. "Or bad storms—whichever comes first!"

"Chief," #4 child—interrupted, "Why don't you build us a bomb shelter like the Clark's? It's neat!"

"Yeah," the chorus rang.

"But they have two children, not *nine!*" I chimed in.

"Can you imagine being trapped in a bomb shelter with nine kids?" #2 child—grimaced.

"Especially if you're the daddy!" Chief chuckled.

"You'd be in good company," my eyes swept the table. "Nothing I like better than my little chicks around me."

"No telephone," #1 child—said, ignoring me.

"Fun," #4 child—giggled.

"Quiet!" #3 child—pleaded. "I'm serious. Chief what do you want us to do? We have to let the school know!"

Chief looked around. "Chances are I'd be at the office. Libbylove will be with the youngest."

Number 8 and 9's eyes swept the long table. Mouths dropped open.

"I'd be at kindergarten," #7 child—#2 daughter—chirped.

"You and I would be at senior high," #1 child said to #2.

"That's okay, Sis. We'd be with friends."

"You and I would be at junior high," #3 said to #4, nodding.

"You two would be at Garrett Grammar School," I said, noting the lost looks they exchanged. They looked at me.

Our minds met. Fire drills, yes. Bomb shelters we never considered.

The children rocked back and forth in their chairs.

"We'd have to build a shelter big enough for lots of rocking chairs," Chief teased. He always threatened to replace our dining room straight chairs.

"Don't forget swinging doors, Chief!" #1 child laughed.

"We'd need a small jail for #8 and 9," #2 child added, "to keep them inside!"

The two little ones beamed at all the attention.

"All kinds of games."

"Books. Lots of books."

"Just need one big bed. We like sleeping together. Especially during storms."

"Wanna' shelter, daddy. Wanna' shelter, daddy," #8 popped up from his seat and ran to Chief.

"Me, too. Me, too," #9 followed suit.

"Quiet. Back to your seats, gentlemen. Finish your supper. Never could afford a shelter big enough for this crew." Chief put a stop to children's hour chatter. "Did we say the blessing?"

"Before you came."

"Say it again. We have a full house tonight—a real blessing. No ball games, music, meetings, babysitting. Join hands! Heads down! No peeking!" Chief barked orders.

Moravian-style hand holding was a ritual we adopted to keep fingers still. Touching has a calming effect.

". . . and thank you for all our many blessings." Chief looked up and down the table, his countdown. "1,2,3,4,5,6. No, once again. 1,2,3,4,6,7,8,9. Now, that's got it. Did I miss anybody?"

"Number 5!" they all boomed.

"Me, daddy," a little voice wavered.

"Come here, Son," Chief took the forgotten number on

his big knee. "You've got to make more noise around here. You might get lost. Speak up."

There was plenty of noise later on. Plenty of speaking up at bedtime. I broke up two pillow fights before escaping to the girls' room.

"It's okay you don't dig Latin, Mom." Number 1 child gave me a good-night hug. "You're a big help with lit."

"Mom, pu-leeze roll my hair!" my youngest daughter begged.

"You're too young," chided my eldest.

"I want curly hair like yours."

"There's nothing prettier than shiny brown hair," I said, stroking her smooth locks.

After finishing the girls' prayers, I rechecked the boys.

"Mom!" I dodged a wash cloth. "Will you please tell that guy to leave my razor alone. He only has two hairs!" #1 son boomed.

"So? Have to shave the two when they get long," #2 son defended himself.

"Mom, will you get #5 to call me early tomorrow?" #3 asked. "He'll listen to you."

"I don't have breakfast," #5 declared. "Number 3 does!"

"Calm down, troops." I lowered my voice. Setting-the-good-example yoke weighed heavily upon me. "You can read the chart."

"I want pancakes tomorrow," #1 son instructed the "breakfast" kid.

"You can have pancakes your week," #3 countered. "I plan this week. It's corn-beef hash!"

"Don't turn that overhead light on to wake me up, please," #5 begged the 'breakfast' kid, who also sounds reveille. "I'd rather have my toe shook and the covers jerked off."

"Mom, can't you do anything about that kid?" #4 asked complainingly. "He sleeps in his clothes half the time."

"He'll get over it," I patted #6, inspecting him. "You did!" I smiled.

"Yeah!" #3 defended his little brother. "I remember when we tried to get you to swim. You wouldn't learn. You yelled, 'I *hate* water! I don't even like to take a *bath!* "

The scuffle began.

"Halt, boys. Join the army. They like a fighting spirit."

"Libbylove," Chief called from downstairs. "Don't take all night!"

"Five down. Two asleep. Two to go!" I yelled back.

I went into the two youngest boys' room. They were waiting, questions ready.

"Mom, is God a woman?" #8 asked.

"A woman?" *Who knows?* I thought. I tucked him in. "What makes you ask?"

"Only 'shes' listen." #8 declared.

"Men listen, too."

"Not Daddy."

"He has so many to listen to all day. At night he's tired of listening. Remember we said, 'Our Father . . .' when we prayed?"

"Libbylove!" Chief again. "Aren't you through yet?"

"Why does he always want you when you're with me?" #8 asked.

"Just seems that way, Son." I gave him another kiss. "You will have a wife someday."

"Can't wait. Then I'll be boss!"

I turned off the lights. Number 9 had conked out.

Downstairs, Chief was stirring up the stacked bills on the desk. They were piled high.

"Where's the plumber's bill?"

"Has his turn come up?" I waded through the stack.

"He said they never had to replace a commode before."

"Don't suppose commode designers expect seven little boys to have a turn rocking back and forth on top." Shaving with their daddy was a morning ritual before they began doing it for real. Each had his turn. Number 8 still has a small scar because he picked up Chief's razor one morning instead of his toy model.

"How did prayers go? Did #8 pray for a bomb shelter?"

"No. But he's not worried. He's prepared."

"How?"

"I cleaned out his treasure chest today. I saw his collection. He calls it his fallout shelter. He's stashed three apples, three plastic forks, two pencils, some dried-up poster paint, two small boxes of his favorite cereal, a toy truck, and three baked sweet potatoes," I said, stuffing the plumber's check I'd written in an envelope.

"What's going on in the adult world?" I asked Chief, who was standing over me, watching.

"Joe's sending Sally to the beach. She needs a rest from a husband, house, and two children."

"I can identify with that. I've got to get a new doctor. One that says I need a rest. Work agrees with me, they say."

"Mom!"

"Thought the children's hour was over," Chief moaned.

". . . but woman's work is never . . ." I went out into the hall. One tiny pajamaed boy poked his face between the banisters.

"Forgot to tell you, Mom. Man stopped me out front today. He was walking. I was playing with my brothers, you know. He said, 'Little boy, how many kids you all got?' When I said, nine, he yelled, *nine!* Should have seen his eyes falling out. Like this, Mom!" His eyes glowed in the dark. "Mom, is nine a lot of kids?"

"According to who's counting, son." I kissed the tip of his nose through the banister. "That's a good question."

"What couldn't keep till morning?" Chief mumbled as I got into bed again.

"Wanted to know if nine was a lot of kids?"

"What did you tell him?"

"After answering fifty-four questions since four this afternoon, I said, 'It's questionable!' "

Like James, I "count it all joy."

15
Children Keep You Young
(or Traveling with the Troops)

"Mom, stop the car! Number 1 son's disappearing! Can't see him! It's my fault, Mom. I was fighting, too. Mom, please!"

Sure enough, he was out of sight. The rearview car mirror showed only the curve of a dusty road. No little boy. After sending up more "Please, God's," I turned the station wagon around. There was #2 child—#1 son—trudging along—hot, dirty, and yes, remorseful.

He would never believe it hurt me more to stop the car and let him out to walk, or that I carefully chose a seldom-traveled road.

"Do you think you can behave now?"

He threw his sweaty body against me. We all smiled through our tears.

"I've told you over and over, I can't drive safely if you are fighting! Will there be any more?"

"No, ma'am. No ma'am," they chorused.

"I can't keep my eyes on the road and you all too. I can't tell who starts the fights. I only know who can finish them—me, the mama. It's my responsibility."

All eyes were riveted on me.

"I *can* leave home. I love you. I think you are fun to be with—a pleasure to take places. You know the difference in indoor behavior and outdoor behavior. Now you know about car behavior. No fighting! When you're all grown, and everyone is more equal in size, you can fight it out. But not around me. And not in the car! Understand?"

They nodded their heads, squirming.

"Any questions?"

Heads shook negatively. They were anxious to get on with it.

"When you all are mamas, you can stop car fighting *your* way."

The little boys giggled at the thought of being mamas.

"We h-a-y-ve, Mom. We h-a-y-ve!"

They kept their promise. The same scene, same script did not have to be repeated for years.

They knew they have alternatives. They could stay home. I wasn't raising public nuisances if I could help it.

Each parent has to decide what he or she can put up with behaviorally in their children. It's a personal deal. Children beg for rules and guidelines. So do I (see Prov. 13:24; Mark 10:14,16). I try to keep no's, rules, lines I draw, to a bare minimum. More range for personal development. It's the best chance for me to be like the famous brokerage house—when Libby speaks, everyone listens. The rewards for good behavior are greater (see 2 Chron. 15:7). It's necessary for mamas to reward children (see Ps. 31:23). There's enough joy to go around. Spread it (see 1 Pet. 4:13).

There were more joys as each child appeared. Child #4—son #3—confessed every time he got off the school bus that there might be another baby in the house. He found joy in confusion. That meant changing rooms, roommates, beds, and routines with each new baby's appearance.

A new baby didn't stop the troops from traveling, merely slowed them down. Through the years I tried every method I heard, read, or thought up to travel with babies. My pediatrician referred patients to talk with me. He didn't have time.

He knew I enjoyed practicing medicine. Traveling with children I knew about. There was no instant everything then.

First I devised a method of transporting baby's bottle needs. That was simple. I put sterilized bottles in a bag and took along small cans of milk. Each feeding time I opened one, added it to the sterilized water mixed with dark, thick, sweet syrup. If time ran out, I'd use the group method—all the sterilized nipples in one bag, sterilized water in a vacuum bottle, and sterilized empty bottles. I was a whiz at formula dispensing, so good an army doctor friend asked my advice. He whispered "constipation"—wanted to know about regulating the doses of thick, sweet syrup to control bowel movements, according to individual needs of babies. He hated to ask another doctor, he confessed.

Chief's preference for nonstop motor trips went eventually down the drain. He had to visit every country store along the well-traveled roads to warm the baby's bottle. He learned to enjoy the different characters hovering around potbellied stoves. I suggested he moonlight as a census taker, or a political pollster. My ideas were not appreciated. I admit I can be ahead of my time.

I was way ahead of time with my first two children—so far ahead they remembered nothing. I took them on boat rides on Mobile Bay, and we toured Bellingrath Gardens. They remembered not a glimmer. Only a well-known child-rearing book saved me. After that I had a slight idea of what to expect.

At least I knew what to expect when we traveled with Chief. He only travels to get where he's going. He was most patient on long trips from Alabama to North Carolina. After all we were going to see our mamas—his favorite people, thank God. (Chief certainly has made *me* one!') The trip home was testy, but not because of numbers. We only had two children then. It was because Chief was in his nonstop theory stage. I had to crawl from the back seat to the front and back again, taking care of children—pregnant or not! We found a baby's bed that could be attached to the back of front seat. Joy. Relief. It was not all pain. Discovered memory was coming to #1 child.

We had car trouble in a town halfway home. Finally arriving, we stayed in Carolina a week. We came back through the same town at night. The car was now in good shape. Number 1 jumped up, pointed all around the town, exclaiming, "Car fix! Car fix!" The first signs of intellect or memory still thrill me. It's a time of thanksgiving (see 1 Tim. 4:3).

There were many times of thanksgiving through the years, traveling with the troops, especially when Chief would stop the car to let them run. Every game, every song, every riddle, every joke, every story had been used. Every minute was a challenge.

It was some kind of challenge trying to find lactic acid milk once. We usually made our own. Then it appeared on the market. But not always. They didn't have it when we ran out at midnight, at the beach—vacation time. It changed our life-style. That was the end of vacations at the beach with children.

Very dutifully Chief through the years had brought the tribe to the beach. He complained about sand in the bed, salt in the eyes, and sunburn on the feet. Nothing was right. Having to scour the beach for milk at midnight did it. Prayerfully I pointed out to him the foolishness of spending money and precious vacation time being miserable. I would escort the troops to the beach. He could come weekends if he wanted to. Secretly we thought he was a poor sport. Years later he learned how allergic he was to the sun; we learned how wrong it is to be judgmental.

Our vacation days in the sun were enjoyable but incomplete. We all missed Chief, especially me. The children's job was to keep me happy, especially at homecoming time—Nightfall. It was comforting to know I had the go-ahead to call him if I were too homesick. I even conquered that. I sneaked one of his T-shirts to sleep with. That solved the problem. I could sleep like a log next to his special shirt he's worn. I goofed only once. Couldn't find anything he'd left behind except a dirty sock! We learned carrying a friend for me to play with worked best. I was lucky enough to have a few crazies who loved traveling with the troops, especially to the beach.

The beach was wide enough in the Carolinas for our crowd. There were enough dunes for boys. These were unforgettable days: long stretches of getting-acquainted time; no car pools, lessons, or chores; opportunities for long walks with a teen. There were lots of chances to answer questions. "Why did you marry Chief?" "Tell me about falling in love. Will I?" "Tell me about Uncle Willie?" "Will I be fat like Aunt Sara when I grow up?" "Can they really read each other's minds?" "Tell me about your mom's courtship in buggy days."

Sometimes there were one-on-one sessions, sometimes togetherness. They liked togetherness then. If riding through a town and we hit a stoplight, they'd shake the younger sleeping ones.

"Sit up. Sit up and be counted!"

They delighted in the reactions of bored adults who glanced their way. Bystanders' eyes popped out when they saw our car and counted heads. If they couldn't awaken a sleepyhead, the older kids would oblige the car next to us by holding up nine fingers. So accustomed to attention, they usually missed the stares when we toured on foot. They didn't even see the double takes when #9 son dragged his stuffed lion to the Washington (D.C.) Zoo. It was as big as he. His brothers understood. He wanted to see the reaction of the real lions.

No one looked up when the chef at a Gettysburg, Pennsylvania, restaurant brought the two youngest back from the kitchen. They were too impressed by his billowy white hat. They didn't hear, "I've never had anyone come into my kitchen and thank me for being a 'good cooker.' " After all, we always told them to thank the cooks along the way.

Yes, we had a few invitations that included "family." Memorable. And few. A mountain hostess friend couldn't wait to see if she could feed and house us all for a weekend. Every detail had been thought of—beds and cots down halls, ample food cooked in canning pots, a cue from me. We had a bundle of laughs, especially her cautionary move of rolls of plastic on the rugs. She learned she could handle eleven extras. The children learned every hump is not a mountain. Cattle don't fall off hillsides. Tall trees do not pierce the moon. Mountains don't all look alike.

They were impressed, especially by our hostess who gave them undivided attention—her brilliant smile, her lyrical laugh. They dubbed her "Pretty Lady." She considered that her reward.

Sometimes the children rewarded our hosts by renaming things. Like "Lane's Lake." It's "Kerr Lake" on the map. That matters not. The troops appreciated the annual invitation to spend the rare day at the lake. Their host patiently taught them to water ski. The hostess filled the bottomless stomach pits with delicious food. They never ran out of food or compliments. "We'd rather have you and your nine than some with their one!" That was our reward.

All traveling with the troops was not out of town. When Chief would take off for the golf course, I'd light out with the troops. We had been cooped up all week. We'd pack a wagon with a picnic, blankets, and books when there were two or three of us. We'd walk to the nearest beauty spot for fun and fellowship, take turns reading aloud or to ourselves. The boys climbed trees, flew kites, or explored.

Exploring became more popular as they grew older. We'd pile in the car and take off for surrounding historic spots. We swapped stories about the olden days. We'd see who could find the most interesting tombstone—check their ages, the stories of their lives. Broken heart? Childbirth? War? What was it like then? Furniture? Any around now?

That precipitated an antique junket. We had our favorites, because we were welcomed. The once-nervous owner knew the troops had to cram their little paws in their pockets, keep their elbows close to their sides, and pay for broken goods. They never had to. They enjoyed listening to the history of a clock or sword. The buddy system was employed at all times.

As they left the nest to take babysitting, grass-cutting, or store clerking jobs, they still had their buddy. There were always others to inherit their window or look after "his charge." They took great pride in "their child's behavior." After an outing the older offspring always checked. They never wanted a bad report.

Bad reports were few. There was grumbling, yes, especially at school, church, or civic-club picnics. I dressed them all alike. They hated it: Not all—just the older ones. Meanest Mama! How could anyone who stressed individuality insist on conformity of dress? It was a simple survival tactic. With children swarming over the place, they all looked alike. At a glance I could tell who was in a ditch, up a tree, or in a fight. It had better not be one in a red-and-yellow plaid top and khaki bottom. I never had to open my mouth. A glance checked their behavior. I read them. They read me. They knew if I was happy, anxious, irritated, relaxed, or nervous. It was mutual.

I get excited a lot, but rarely nervous. Lightning sometimes scares me; rides at fairs, always. I try not to show it. But I can't fool them. I don't say anything but I identify. I remember at the World's Fair in New York in 1964 my youngest insisted on riding an innocent-looking train. The ride would slow down. He'd start to get out. It would start again with a jerk. "Holy Toledo!" he shouted. I understood. You can learn the negative things you have in common with your children, as well as the positive. Share a prayer lesson opportunity.

Chief always used traveling with the tribe as a learning opportunity. While traveling from point to point, he had a captive audience with whom to get his point across. The first time one of our children defended his "average" school grades. Chief took the long way home from church. He took them through sections of town where "national average" people live. That took care of their contentment to be average.

Sometimes Chief carried them on an appreciation tour. When complaints rang, "We're the only kids our age that *have* to work," he knew the cure. When "It's a privilege to work" fell on deaf ears, he knew how to improve their hearing. There's a lot of repetition with nine. Sharing a Sunday-afternoon ride with a child on crutches, who was far from home, cured their discontent. Triggered more fervent "Thanks, Dear Lord" in us. Our local Cerebral Palsy Hospital has done more for us than we could ever do for it. It has made us appreciate ball games more—just being able to move.

Baseball games were fun and high on the outdoor-behavior list. You could holler as loud and long as possible. Indians that could not sit could run behind the stands until they dropped. There was no nagging for food or drink. Chief took care of that. They could get something when the numbers were under 5 on the scoreboard. That kept them looking at the scoreboard. They never had to ask the score. They knew when foodtime was acceptable. Having no junk food at home made excursions more pleasurable.

Child #8—son #7—spent his time and energy collecting programs, his pleasure. Everywhere he went it was the same, recitals or graduations. He lugged home all his little arms could carry. They joined his collection of doorstops in his treasure chest. It was the greatest collection east of the Mississippi. Took him months finally to unscrew all the doorstops in our new home. He never asked anyone else to help, never asked anyone to carry programs for him. No one laughed, especially now. He moved through the years from doorstops to coins. Traveling with the troops paid off for him.

Traveling is contagious. We have had a good case of it. All my troops want to know what's on the other side of the mountain. Some would rather you tell them. Most have amply used their opportunities. They've joined any group or club that went places. Some are more adventurous than others. They appreciate explorers, ancestors, and those who dared to leave the familiar. They are the ones who learned that God is everywhere (see Ps. 65:8). We're safe everywhere in God's hands.

16
Runaway Slaves
(or Surviving Four Teenagers at a Time)

"Don't worry," I smilingly reassured two of my little boys. "Number 1 son's leaving home again!" They smiled at each other.

"How many times has he left home, Mom?"

"Lost count."

"Sounded like he fell out of bed," one commented.

"Bet he got knocked out!" the other joined in.

"Put your knives up, boys. You know I don't allow talking about each other. If you can't say something nice . . ."

"Sure, Mom, we know: 'Don't say anything.' "

"Right!" I plopped a thermometer in one mouth, thrust funnies in the other boy's hand. Kept right on silently praying, "Keep me calm, dear Lord. Balanced. Fair. Pleasant."

The Sunday Special was limping along this Sunday. There were two sick ones to be taken to the doctor. Number 1 son was balking at having to go to church. This was a new development. He had had fun at choir camp. *Seventeen years perfect attendance in church ought to be honored, I rationalized.* I reviewed the revolting revolt: It was expected, normal, and not pleasurable.

"Lazy teenagers!" Chief stormed. "I called that boy once. When I went *back* upstairs to check on the others, he was still in bed. Have to leave him. We'll be late. You'd better hurry to the doctor's. Don't worry about #1 son. I'll campus him!"

Chief's eyes awaited my reaction. Condemnation? Approval? Being "campused" is the hardest. I'm the jailer (see Prov. 4:3,4; 6:9-11).

"No other Chief could find such understanding," I assured him. I hugged him.

"We're ready, Chief!" #1 daughter announced. "Need any help with the sick ones, Mom?" No mention of the noisy struggle upstairs.

"Like Henny Penny, did you think the sky was falling?" I looked at my eldest. College would be a retreat for her after Bedlam. She was cool, calm, and collected—born that way.

"Don't worry 'bout that sky falling, Mom," she laughed. "It hasn't yet. Worry about being late. Do we always have to be late?"

Moving troops is never easy. I watched part of my family pile into the car, the littlest jostling for windows, the middle ones sitting up straight to preserve Sunday neatness. Chief looked lost. He always did when part of his tribe was missing.

I went upstairs to check on the campused one.

"Get out of here!" #1 son's words attacked me. The coffee cup rattled. The funnies I brought floated downward. "I don't want to hear a thing you have to say." Instead of a puddle of complaints, I was facing a sulking lion, licking his wounds, anxious to pounce on any intruder—especially a Meanest Mama.

I lowered the coffee to a safe place, retrieved the funnies. I respected his mood—didn't touch him or say a word.

"No need to bring peace offerings!" I shrugged.

I went out the door. "I'm really leaving for good this time!" he called after me.

The door closed, I breathed a sigh of relief. I sent up several "Thank you's." Everything was normal—threatening.

I checked on my two sick ones. No temperature taking this time. There were more interesting things going on. They forgot to make a production of their state of health.

"Put that thermometer back in your mouth. If you don't conform, you'll get the same as #1 son!"

"That was pretty silly, hiding in the bathroom at church last Sunday."

"Yeah. Talking with his buddies."

"We all do silly things, boy," I answered as I put on their bathrobes. They didn't beg for a raincoat to go over them. "You played football in the cold rain. Got sick." I shoved bedroom shoes toward them. "I don't rest enough."

"Okay, Mom. We *know*."

No sounds came from #1 son's room. I ushered the sick ones to the car. *Hands off,* I thought, but my heart and prayers went out to him. It's pretty trying to be seventeen, the oldest of seven boys. He thought fifteen was the pits, being too young to drive. Setting the good example gets old. *For the mother. For the father,* I thought, checking his money. He never could keep enough. The inevitable prescription for everything (see John 6:9).

Midday lunch was like a wake. Number 1 son's absence was a dagger hanging overhead. All felt it acutely. Even the blessing fell flat. Chief retreated to the golf course. The youngest napped. The two sick ones sank into a feverish sleep. The middle ones worked on their tree camp. I insisted on doing the dishes. There were no complaints from #1 child. I needed more prayer time (see Matt. 11:28).

After a comforting session, I saw things in their right perspective. I reviewed the crazy running-away times of #1 son. As a preschooler, he had packed a bag larger than he. He was back in an hour, inquiring of his family status, seeking reassurance. The Juggling Jester was a real amateur then. I sought balance between overreacting and being over-protective. Cause and effect. The second time, as a grammar-schooler, he hid in an abandoned barn nearby. He slipped back into his room at bedtime. Chief restrained me from showing undue concern. Males understand other males. I gave #1 son an extra hug later that night. I thought he was sleeping. He pulled me back down for a "forgive-me" kiss. No words were necessary.

At thirteen he had hid out at his grandparents'. A phone call cleared that mystery. At sixteen, he spent the night at a funeral home. A friend working there couldn't persuade him to stay. Number 1 son was scared enough to walk home alone at three in the morning. Since seventeen, he had visited recruiting offices regularly. They assured him Uncle Sam would call when he was needed.

I got his number early. Number 1 son didn't even want to go to camp, swore he walked in his sleep. Wouldn't want my child to walk into the lake, would I? *He did have a pattern of sleepwalking, I rationalized.* He lasted one week at camp. I soon learned he was a home-by-nightfall body.

It was a long week. "Campused" one spent spare time in his room. He was an avid reader. On Saturday, we didn't mention the Friday night basketball game. Usually there would be an animated basketball discussion. We talked only about our favorite team North Carolina, which was in the national finals. The tension was relieved by a laugh provided by #6 boy, all of seven then. UCLA was favored in the tournament. Our team's chances looked slim.

"Don't worry, you all. I have a friend that has a friend that says UCLA means 'You can lose also!' "

That brought a welcomed mood change. Number 6 son beamed his appreciation of being front and center—a rare event for him. Not that he didn't make attempts. He never could get that much undivided attention in Bouncing Bedlam.

Nothing seems enjoyable in Bedlam when one cog is loose in the family wheel. I tried to turn the lemony situation into lemonade with a private discussion on the behavioral effects on others with those capable of understanding. I gave more explanations of differences of father and mother love. I reiterated why we need both.

After supper dishes, the little ones were bedded down. Some played games, others watched television with Chief. I couldn't read. Clicking pool balls in the basement distracted me. Number 1 son was practicing his shots alone. Being gregarious, this hurt.

Flashes of the past week's conversations flooded my mind —outbursts.

"Other parents don't make their children go to church. Not when they're seventeen. Not *every* Sunday. Sick or well. I'm old enough to decide what's best. I'm almost old enough to fight for my country. Jesus went about His own business. He did *His* thing!"

Every outburst was silenced with the hackneyed retort, "As long as you're under this roof you do as Chief says." Sometimes I would try humor, ". . . and what are you going to tell your child when you're a daddy?"

"Not me. I'm taking a slow freighter around the world. No wife. Certainly no big family!"

"Which one do you want to get rid of?"

There was a head-shaking, smile exchange.

"A large family is like an army. We can't have insubordination. It takes teamwork. Spirit. Cooperation. Remember."

"Yeah, I remember. 'Cooperation is doing with a smile what you have to do anyway . . .' " #1 son finished my sentence. Just like Chief!

The Libbynese was interrupted by the doorbell. Number 1 son was saved. Seven of his friends filed in, heads lowered. The bravest spoke up, "About #1 son," he croaked. "We know he's being punished. But we haven't seen him all week. We miss him. Could we please shoot pool with him? Just for a while?"

Chief appeared. "Sounds like a platoon! Go on downstairs, boys. I warn you, #1's been practicing his shots." They thundered down the steps.

"Let's make some fudge!" Chief suggested.

"They might not eat that. Remember their complexions!"

"Make some for me. How about marshmallow squares or roasted peanuts?"

"I still have drinks left from the sick ones. Hide them."

The rest of the children joined us in the kitchen.

"Party?"

"We're showing #1 son you can have fun at home," Chief declared. "Seventeens think you have to spend money."

"We thought he was campused!"

"I said he couldn't go *out!*" Chief said. "I didn't say no one could come *in!*"

"Never understand adults," they mumbled, taking the goodies to the basement.

Our quiet time was ended by the nervous platoon I let in the front door. The now-smiling boys clambered into the kitchen. They were pushing #1 son in front of them.

"This is the best fudge. Melts in your mouth."

"Tell 'em what we said," they kept punching #1 son in the ribs. "'Bout how lucky you are. How swell your folks are."

All eyes were glued to #1 son. He reddened, spluttered. No words came. He couldn't speak. Didn't have to. Love and admiration shone in his eyes. He kept nodding his head vigorously. We exchanged awkward hugs and backslappings.

"Go back to your game, boys. Thanks for coming upstairs."

"I'll never understand adults!" The little boys went back to their games.

I'll never understand children, especially four teenagers at a time. One is bad enough. I hadn't thought too much about it. Just endured it. Number 6 child—#5 son—quietly observed the scene at the supper table. Looked down the sea of faces to me, he declared, "Mom, you have a young teenager, a middleaged teenager, an old teenager, and an ancient teenager."

"Don't remind me," I laughed at his assessment. "I feel bad enough."

I didn't want to complain. I asked for it (see 2 Cor. 8:20). Patience I work on and pray for (see James 5:12,17). In fact, the complaint department was open after school. I listened to all the wrongs of their day. It was feather-smoothing time. If things went too smoothly, it was dull to some, especially #4 child—#3 son. His favorite indoor sport during his old teen years was trying to make me lose my equanimity. If I didn't give him the "Where-when-who-with" treatment, he'd trap me into it.

"Guess where I'm going tonight, Mom?"

"Opera?"

"Sure!"

(Silence.)

"Don't you want to know?"

"You're eighteen. I trust your judgment."

"I'm going to the city."

"Hmm."

"Got the cutest little waitress there!"

"I bet!"

"Oldern' I am."

"Hmm."

"She's got three kids!"

"Sure!"

"We're gonna' share a fifth and smoke some . . ."

"Get outta' here!" I threw something at him. "You never get too old for me to spank!" If I caught him, I placed a tap where God provided (see Prov. 13:24). Our little drama included an exchange of hugs. He feigned disappointment.

"Gee, Mom, I thought you didn't care anymore! Took me almost five minutes to get a rise outta' you!"

Even teenagers respect discipline. They sense it's a special kind of attention. Without it, love and respect fly out the window. If you don't respect your own rights, you may neglect the rights of others.

Not only do I have the right to discipline, I have the duty (see Deut. 4:10; Judg. 13:8; Col. 3:16). Discipline is setting the good example. It's not an overnight accomplishment. It starts from the cradle. The teen years are difficult to backtrack or catch up. It scares you when you realize that you have, according to experts, been molded, taught, and influenced about all you can by age six. By the time our children were six they'd learned charm. I had tried to teach them not to ask for anything when visiting, to give the other person opportunities to be generous.

Number 2 child wasn't so sure he could buy that theory. The next-door neighbors invited him inside. They said he admired a bowl of apples. He solemnly declared to the host, "Mr. Merill, if *I* was a big man, and *you* were a little boy visiting at *my* house, I'd ask *you* to have an apple!"

Not all my children were charm buckets. Tempers were evident. I had never seen a temper tantrum, only heard about them. The first trick pulling I witnessed, I used the shock treatment by instinct. A few drops of ice water in the face got a reaction—up and off the floor, sputtering. With no sympathy, no audience, there was no reason to continue the act.

Was that cruel? It's a matter of opinion. The Jesting Juggler figured it was not as cruel as letting the behavior be blessed by default—doing nothing. If I permitted their temper tantrums, tirades, whining, crying, bribing, pouting, not to mention more serious offenses of lying and stealing, I would cheat everybody—myself, my children, and society. What is termed "cute" at one age is disastrous at another. It multiplies. I know something about multiplication. It compounds things.

Matters constantly have to be balanced. The Jesting Juggler sought to find the fine line between showing too much concern and too little, being too strict and too lenient, knowing when to hold tight and when to let go.

Whether it's letting a little one lick the spoon or enjoy some candy for making it to the potty, most of us respond to rewards. We learn cause and effect. Rewarded for good behavior, mine were more apt to repeat it. When punished, they would stop. Some only needed a smile or hug reward. Some only needed a "drop-dead" look. All were individuals. The message moves up and down the ranks in a big family. News travels.

Children prefer love. You can't spoil a child by loving him too much. Affection (a treat, surprise, or some extra privilege) makes life more pleasureable all around. Some parents meet their children's financial needs and starve their emotional ones. Maybe because the Peter-Paul Principle hung around our house, I ignored their financial needs, if possible. Didn't want them to suffer the shock from a moneyed world like I did. More money takes more work.

Work is an humbling experience, a necessity. The best teacher is necessity. Every child needs work to help him come to realistic terms. Work supports your habits whether it is gas, food, or a roof over the head. If freely given, it robs a child of pressure and incentive for essential needs. With no pressures, then they don't see the necessity of getting on with their own lives, of growing up.

Growing up is what most every teen looks forward to—especially flying the coop. The dear Lord, Master of Timing, knows it is mutual, especially when you have four teenagers at a time. He promises to help us keep our minds (see 1. Tim 1:7).

Survival techniques? Trust in the Lord. He gives his Spirit of power and of love (see 1. Tim. 1:7). Never quit praising, showing affection. It proves to your offspring that they are lovable—a must.

17
Rebellion Residues
(or Life from the Bottom of the Clothes Pile)

"Hey, Hey, whadda' ya' say? Grab those dishes and come this way!"

"Cut it out, Mom!"

"You're glued to the tube. Thought I'd speak to you in terms you understand."

Silence. All eyes were on the televised ball game. I had no diapers to change, no mouths to feed. How did I get to be a displaced person in my own home?

"I'm running away!"

"Don't pay any attention to her. It's just the stage she's in!"

I slammed the door. No one noticed. Stomping down the street I thought of the sign I had seen, "Avenge yourself, live long enough to be a problem to your children!" I'm working on it.

Where did I go wrong? Was it the democratic system I used at family meetings? Now I'm outvoted. I've lost my bargaining power. Once I could influence a vote or two, almost, until #1 son came home unexpectedly from college. Can I help it if he brought a friend? Who expects company at 3:30 in the afternoon? I was dressed in silver from head to toe. That wasn't so easy. Silver spray on hair. Silver lamé dress, sparkly hose, silver shoes. The works. It was a dress rehearsal. There was a costume party that night—my night out.

Where was #1 son's sense of humor? Good thing Chief didn't appear in his silver satin jump suit. The funnel for a hat was a Wizard of Oz steal. Complains about having a hard time explaining his mama, does he? Turn about is fair play. He should know the Bedlam bunch by now. (He used to be one of us.)

I remember #1 son's first sign of losing his sense of humor. It was at an Easter party. I was on the planning committee. Live chickens let loose among the crowd wasn't accepted. What about Chief as Daddy Rabbit? Me as Mama? We had costumes that were dull—not enough pizzazz. How about nine little rabbits hopping along behind us? Terrific. Band playing, "Here Comes Peter Cottontail!"

I don't know who the killjoy was. Number 1 girl—#1 child—having to fasten all those yarn tails on wiggling children? Couldn't be #2 child—#1 son. He got to chauffer them. I thought he'd do anything to get to drive Chief's car! Besides, they all got hugs, kisses, ice cream, and a year's subscription to *Mad* magazine! Rebellion? Not that night.

I'm the one that should have rebelled. Four carpools a day! It was hard to keep them all straight. I got out of them to drive my own. To use a country expression; "I used to meet myself coming and going in the road." It still shakes me when I see a car like mine, especially full of children. I think, *this is it! Do they have Scouts, music, or choir today?*

It's my own fault. There was my driving-age child out working, from my insistence on learning the outside world. To heck with the home front. I've been deserted. After all, didn't I teach them to sweep, mop ad nauseam? Simon Legree isn't the prettiest name. It almost replaced Meanest Mama. I'm proud none have been fired yet. Bosses like them. The kids like the money they earn. I don't like borrowing from them. A switch.

Why can't they be sloppy like other teenagers? They're all neatnicks. They take more baths. No more four in the tub. They're only interested in private property—what's mine, what's yours. I only have myself to blame. Each one had their own chest of drawers. I didn't have one until I hit college.

Spring was chest-of-drawer-painting time. I painted each offspring's name on theirs. It mattered not they couldn't read. Might help them learn. Each drawer's contents were pictured outside. I drew clothes hanging on a clothesline that hung from knob to knob. As they grew older, just words adorned the drawers. Didn't want to insult their reading ability.

Did it work? Rarely. Coat hangers dangled lonesomely in closets. Drawers were almost empty. Kids did inherit the painting jobs. They enjoyed learning. Sand from the nearby sandpile put an end to my encouraging budding Rembrandts.

Treasures I understood. I have a few, most of whom are two-legged. I saw to it each child had his little trunk of possessions. As he aged, he acquired a GI trunk or reasonable facsimile. Possessions and dirty clothes often swapped places. One man's treasure is another man's trash. Never adept at telling the difference, I let it be. I was outnumbered. Once when one son was mad at the Meanest Mama, he threw all his clean clothes out of his chest of drawers onto Stone Mountain—my clothes pile. It was an exercise in futility when he realized he washed his own anyway. Stone Mountain never went away—no matter what. The Health Department never closed us down.

There had to be an answer to the clothes pile problem. Chief and I spied some cotton-picking baskets in South

Carolina. Huge and sturdy, they ought to do it. We purchased one for each child and attached his name. No more excuses. As soon as they knew the difference between "on and off," "light and dark," the laundry chores lightened. Now the responsibility for lipsticks, pens, frogs, and rocks left in pockets was theirs. Money was different. The one adept at undoing the washer trap got the money. It was cheaper than repairmen. It acquainted them with the ancient apprenticeship system—learning by doing—after much watching.

Did the baskets solve the problem? They helped immensely. With so many of the same sex, it was difficult for each to know his own clothes. With a basket of his own, it was easier. It was fairly simple when I had three or four. One would have a stripe, or special color or some identifying feature. As the family increased, so did the difficulty in distinguishing characteristics.

White socks did it. Everybody had to have white socks. My Libbynese went unappreciated. "Nobody wears white socks unless they're from the old country," "Nobody wears white socks unless they have athlete's foot!" only brought dirty looks. They learned from me. White socks were *in.* That let me *out.* I never joined in the search for the right length or fit. They were on their own. I did provide a couple of "lost-and-found" baskets—one for unclaimed underwear, the other for socks. The basket with a "mending" sign attached was really the lost-and-found department. They swore I was waiting for the clothes to go out of style so I wouldn't have to mend them.

I had to mend my ways. I remembered my mom's reaction to "Sloppy Joe" sweaters. They had a high neck that fell straight and loose below your waistline. A string of pearls was a must.

"You have a tiny waist. Why hide it?" she'd say. "Why

don't you wear the locket I gave you? It was your grandmother's. Do you have to look like everyone else? Even if it looks terrible on you? Saw you rubbing dirt over those new saddle shoes you persuaded me to buy. Dirt belongs in plowed fields. You are somebody. Why don't you dress like somebody?"

The dirty saddle oxfords of #1 girl I understood. Her crinolines I couldn't fathom. The proportions were so wrong. How did they get between desks? Those long skirts and flat shoes were unflattering to the legs. Mom forgive me (see Eph. 6:2). She told me how little human nature changes; saw good in all things (see Col. 1:10). Rebellion she understood.

Rebellion is so commonplace now, it has lost its zip, touch, and effectiveness. It was an attention-getter once. Now it is so commonplace, it is taken for granted. Conforming is conforming to rebellion. You see it in literature. Writing is no longer judged by cleverness with words, artistic description, building suspense, or plucking the heartstrings. Now words are desecrated, meanings changed. They are used to dig up the most dirt, report the repulsive, offend. That takes no imagination, no brain strain. The choice is ours. Take it or leave it. We're a part and parcel of all we see, so don't put trash in. Trash will come out (see Matt. 15:11). The Good Book tells us what manner of people we should be.

Music lovers we should be. But we have to listen to some dull, repetitive sounds. Our ears are assaulted. We ride by buildings that could be anything from a law office to a private home. Built, of course, on a lot where an old landmark home stood proudly. We have to wear clothes that are uncomfortable, especially shoes. Designers must hate women. We still have the choice (see Luke 12:28; 1 Tim. 6:8).

Rebellion today is really passé. Every good and decent thing has been attacked, ridiculed, and degraded. Why? To be different? If you really want to be different, be a rebel against evil, against ugliness of all kinds.

I hurried home. I couldn't wait to spout my latest Libbynese. Tell my children that if they really wanted to be different, to smile. Everyone will wonder what you're up to. Be kind, and they'll wonder what job you're out to get. Be good to yourself healthwise. Be full of energy and enthusiasm—and everyone will hate you for sure. Or choose to be lazy, dreamy, or contemplative. Will they mistake you for a great thinker? They're certainly different from most people. Rare! Be generous and someone might call the IRS. Be frugal. Your financial condition becomes a topic of conversation. Pay cash. Few know what it looks like in this credit-card age. Be content with being a male or female. They think you've visited a "shrink," a status symbol. Try walking. They'll think your car's been repossessed. Shoe repairmen will eat again. Cut your hair so barbers have money to pass along. Why hide those good looks? (see Isa. 52:7; Rom. 10:15).

Like a new kick? Love your enemy. It'll worry him to death. Like to be alone? Here's Libby's surefire recipe: Don't complain; don't play the gossip game; be a happy person. Some people will leave you alone. They'll think you're nuts (see Rom. 14:22). When the boss blesses you out, grin (see Matt. 5:39; Luke 6:29).

Like challenges? Try loving your neighbor. Like reforming things? Instead of the nation, your friends, relatives, and neighbors, how about yourself? I'm going to start right now —all over again. I'm going back into that house and dish out hugs, whether they want them or not. I'm going to love—my God, my husband, children, friends, even my relatives, and inlaws. Even those who don't think and act like I think they should.

Try to see good in all things (see Rom. 8:28). Don't be

hypocritical (see Luke 11:44). You might even love yourself more. God does (see John 15:13). He sent his own Son (see Rom. 8:3) to show us how to live more abundant lives.

I couldn't wait to get home to my abundant life: My husband; my nine children. I still have to hang in there, to try to set the good example. With God's continuing help I can (see Eph. 3:19-20). I can't wait to try again (see Romans 10:9-10). I can't wait to love my children (see Prov. 4:3-4), love my husband (see Eph. 5:2). The Good Book tells us how to love (1 Cor. 13:5), how to enjoy (1 Tim. 6:17), how to be content (Eph. 4:11)—even in the bottom of a clothes pile!

18
The Strange Loves of a Housewife
(or Foraging in the Outside World)

"Please, ma'am! Don't *say* that! Don't change dairies!"

Tears streamed down his face. Why me? Why couldn't Chief tell him? Why did I have to handle these things?

"Isn't our service satisfactory? Our milk good?"

"Yes, yes," I assured the distraught man.

"Don't understand. You're my biggest account!"

"Please don't take it personally." I patted his arm. "Chief wanted to make a change. We're moving from this Psychiatric Saltbox to Trinity Treat."

"I still don't understand. It's still on my route!"

"It's business. We're switching to the other dairy because their president and his family are Chief's dental patients."

The milkman looked forlorn.

"You've been so kind. I appreciate everything. It's not your fault, or mine. I'm truly sorry. Let's be friends."

He looked at me understandingly, and shook my hand.

The merchants, bakers, and candlestick makers are all part of my life. A mother of nine rarely sees anyone else. They may be the only adults she sees for stretches of time.

My milkman's heart was broken. I understood. We consumed at least eight quarts a day. He was so kind and patient. But there are other milkmen. The next one was even better. He brought the milk in its case, put it in the refrigerator for me. It wasn't pity, even if I was always pregnant. He just hated to see the beautiful white stuff flowing on the floors. It gave us time to discuss our favorite ball team—another treasured contact with the outside world. Sure I loved my milkman. Number 3 child—#2 son—worked at the dairy when he was older. He was an ice-cream lover like his Mom.

Grocers were fatally attracted to me—couldn't do enough to please me. I ate up this Queen treatment. I knew it wasn't my charm or my looks. It was the totaled bill. A typical breakfast for the eleven of us meant a quart of orange juice, a pound of bacon, a loaf of bread and one-and-a-half dozen eggs. There are seven days in the week still. They haven't changed that. Three loaves of bread were needed per day—not counting biscuits, cornbread, or rolls. Afternoon snacks took tons of peanut butter and jelly. Cereal boxes filled one cabinet. Hot milk cakes were the favorite after-school snacks. Our food was full of surprises, full of anything I could find to throw in—fruit, candy, or nuts. There was never an iced cake. They'd eat the icing and leave the cake.

Naturally the grocer was one of my biggest fans. The only thing he couldn't understand was my fickleness. I didn't come in at the same time, on the same day, like his other customers. I traded wherever the carpool took me. I had grocer friends all over town. One waylaid me one day.

"Where have you been? I've missed you! I got you out of here fast as I could last time. Didn't you make carpool pick-up in time? What's the problem? Aren't the clerks civil?"

"Everything's fine. There aren't as many carpools in summer as in winter. Number 6 child got a job up the street, bagging groceries. I trade there now if I'm out this way."

"Why didn't you send him down here? I'd gladly have hired him."

"Thanks. This son got the job on his own. First store he came to."

"Don't forget me! I'll never forget you!"

There's no way I'll forget minimum five-pound roasts, now up to ten, hamburger galore, two chickens a meal, and eight pounds of butter beans.

I'm unforgettable. It's not exactly the way I planned it. You get your gifts where they're given.

One mailman considered giving in his resignation years before retirement years. He had his reasons. I didn't know until he told me.

"Been delivering your mail a couple of years now."

"Yes you have." *No wonder the children dubbed him "Mr. Grouch,"* I thought. *A smile would crack his face!*

"I thought it was sweet for the little ones to put flowers in the mailbox for me. Presents. Surprises. The cookies were great. I didn't even mind the sticks or stones. No problem. But hereafter would you please check the mailbox before delivery time?"

"Why?"

"Today a kitten jumped out in my face! My nerves are shot!"

No wonder our mailman rarely smiled. In fact I don't endear myself to the Post Office Department. We wade through tons of junk mail. I vigilantly case the mailbox. They have to be watched. My young entrepreneurs answered all ads. They sold everything from newspapers to birthday cards. That was okay. But nothing upset me more than to discover name-selling. I've spent years waylaying envelopes from a certain "boutique" in Hollywood, California. You don't have to be very bright to figure that one out. Porn pushers I'd like to punish. Mere nudes are bad enough, but perversion is a different story. Trying to protect your offspring from fast-buck con artists, drug dealers, and porn merchants is more than a one-woman job. We need all Meanest Mamas.

Repairmen never thought I was a Meanest Mama. They were welcomed. They wore fascinating outfits, had trucks full of interesting things, were never in a hurry, and they always brought a buddy. If they tired of little helpers, they never mentioned it. Expensive built-in entertainment. They loved being offered ice water. A small-fry ritual in our house. Every workman was taken ice water.

Repairmen cleared up lots of household mysteries. So that's what happened to the jackrocks—in the washing machine trap. They were a regular lost-and-found department for rubberbands in the garbage disposal, nut picks lodged in the dishwasher drain, and toothbrushes in commodes. Repairmen replaced worn-out belts and motors regularly. They were always polite, patient, and pointing out that *no* manufacturer expected such wear and tear on their product. One repairman recommended commercial-size appliances.

That guy had watched me go around Stone Mountain for years. He repaired both my washing machine and my spirits, too. He was sympathetic. The more I washed, the larger the washpile. The clothes propagated. Another kid moved in and nobody told me. Once I did laundry count: thirty-five shirts to "do up." Twenty-five white ones went to the laundry. (I had too many troubles with birds flying over the clothesline or kids taking short cuts through the sheets). Seventeen pairs of pants were retrieved from the top of Stone Mountain. Seven needed the cleaners. Ten more were hiding in the mending basket. Nobody was looking for them. They had no knees, were too short or too long. Annually I took a load to the neighborhood laundry, determined to get a fresh start. No dirty clothes lurking in corners or closets! No Stone Mountain! For one day. The laundry bill looked like the national debt. The laundryman loved me.

Even the pool players loved me. No clothes spilling over on the table nearby. The family voted to move the washer and dryer to the back porch and enclose it. We lost a great summer eating spot, but found another catchall. We also found more built-in entertainment: construction men, electricians. Shelves were built to fit the cotton-picking baskets. Gone was my clothes chute idea. It didn't work. I had gone full circle—from individual clothes baskets to bathroom hampers to clothes chute to individual baskets again. Each person assuming his own laundry responsibility is the way to survival for housewives.

Some of my housewifely ideas did work. A built-in ladder in the boy's bathroom reached from floor to ceiling. It held towels most of the time and was a great toy. Handmade, it survived. Pullout drawers built under the bottom of the lavatory cabinets worked well. They were upside down, providing a step-up for little folks. The drawer with lock and key didn't prove practical. Medicines were never stored there. It was a great idea, but I couldn't keep up with the key. Stepstools beside the boy's commode were sensible but not foolproof. The sign I made with a toy gun tacked on it helped the most. "We aim to keep this place clean. Your aim will help."

I welcomed ideas for making life with eleven easier. So were salesmen. They are a challenge. A go-ahead-and-convince-me game is fun, comparing sales pitches, observing different best-foot-forward ways. I was keenly aware of their anxiety to make a sale. It was not solely for profit, but a chance to say to future prospects, "I sold a mother of nine this. She wouldn't be without it!"

I wanted to make a responsible choice. Not all of my choices were good or right, just mine. I foolishly turned down double ovens because of a salesman's condescending attitude. I didn't buy single-unit appliances. I bought a built-in job that was harder to repair. I liked the color—dumb of me! The salesman who tried to warn me was so nice. He helped me shell butter beans. Others sometimes rode along with us on our carpools. There's not much spare time in Bedlam.

I'm glad I took the time to listen to the intercom salesman. It's a joy, especially the speaker in the baby's room that turns on automatically at his cry. A real step saver. The novelty of kids talking to one another in their rooms soon wore off when they learned it was two-way. I could listen to them. You learn more by eavesdropping. Some intercoms were free. The abandoned clothes chute became an innocent-looking listening station, especially from the second floor to the basement. The first floor heating vent was a direct line. You always knew who was doing what, or planning to, or what planning stage they were in. Like my intercom system, my children never let me down. It wasn't perfect, but good.

Good times were shopping times. Each child had a day in the week that was theirs, that is until I ran out of days. All shopping needs were met. It was a fun time together. Soon the older one's idea of fun became something else. They worked as soon as the law allowed. Bought their own turn-ons. Through the years I've used many shopping methods. One made me the star of the show. It took prior preparation. I'd check out the stores by telephone or ads to find the best buy, the most room, patient clerks, and the store's slack time. I'd load the troops in the car for one-shot shopping—shoe day, clothes day, school supplies day. We made many a clerk "Salesman of the Year" or "Queen for a Day." The only complaint from the troops was dressing alike to shop. A troops-dress-alike sales pitch went unappreciated. A sinful banana split made their stares more bearable. At least we got the shopping over with that day.

School supplies day was unforgettable. I accused mine of selling notebook paper to their friends. It disappeared overnight, usually to their hiding places. Number 9 child—#8 son—had logged so much time tagging along as a preschooler, by the time he was of working age, the store hired him. Where else could his employer find anyone as familiar with the stock and who was nicknamed "Bookie?" Before he could walk or talk, he carried books larger than he was. He'd plop down and "read" his book—the only upside-down reader I had. There was one mirror reader but no "I-dare-you-make-me" readers.

The library runs were enjoyable. Enthusiastic readers make it that way. Libraries have everything. They're a great meeting place, resting place, fun place. All except once. My #2 child was making a library run for himself. He didn't think it was much fun working on a term paper. I asked him to bring me a book. I wrote the title and author down for him.

Hours later he stormed in.

"This is the last time, Mom! Never ask again! This is it!"

He threw the book in my lap.

"I told them it wasn't for me. It was for you. They just laughed. I was horrified. The more I said, the worse it got. A mother of nine should be ashamed. From now on, get your own books!"

I had no chance to tell him it wasn't a sex book. At least my library loves had their laugh of the day—Erich Fromm's *The Art of Loving.* Provided me with a much-needed explanation of the different kinds of love, especially the love of a father and mother. I gained knowledge, but lost a library-runner.

Books are splendid companions. One night at the beach, I settled down for my night reading. Child #9 asked to join me. He was a delightful reading companion, even if too young to read. He propped up beside me in bed with his book. No one made fun of his plaid flannel bathrobe. It was too hot for the beach. When he took it off for bed, he removed his possessions from the pocket—small, round puzzle and a letter from me. He could put together the puzzle. He was saving his letter until he could read. It's a real chore to keep your favorite things intact in a big family. You have to carry them on your person. He packed his bag like the rest of the troops—had his own reading material.

"Aren't you glad we like the same thing, Mom?"

"What's that, Son?"

My little three-year-old looked up, smiling. "We both like to read in bed!"

That's one of the joys of a big family. You have so much in common with so many people. I've had common interest with lots of banks and merchants—especially indebtedness. When it's inevitable, enjoy it. We were rugless for years. Stubbornly I stuck to, "I'd rather do without than be saddled with something I don't want." So I did without. I wanted Oriental rugs. Nothing shows. They're childproof. One good financial year we paid a visit to our friendly banker. When a loan amount was discussed, I insisted on a few hundred more. Why? For a trip to see the Big Apple *sans enfant.* If in debt, why not have some memories? They make the paying-back medicine go down easier.

We dropped our little people off in Washington with relatives. Another couple, theater-lovers and good companions, went with us. We caught a matinee and evening performance a day during the Thanksgiving weekend.

That financial manuever was satisfying to all of us—Chief and I, our friends, our little people, our rug man (one each for the living room, den, and entrance hall)—couldn't chance a dining-room rug—and our banker, of course.

My forays into the banking world didn't always bring bliss. Bankers will talk to you. Once, unhappy over an ugly letter sent about an overdue account, I paid a visit to my banker friend, letter in my hand. I doubt there will be a clean financial slate until they all leave the nest.

"Would you rather I go to Friendly Finance or Loan Shark Lane?" I know how to hurt bankers. "I understand Corner Currency will lend anybody any amount anytime!"

Did I get attention? Pronto! He read the letter I had brought.

"Just a form letter. I send them all the time."

"Which place do you recommend?" I persisted. "Paying cash for some items and charging others at the same store is for the birds. We have credit except if we charge. Naturally our bills are large. We're a large family. Multiply like we do, have no understanding. We don't deal with those kind."

After simmering me down, the banker friend started to fill out an application. When I found out I couldn't borrow under my own name, I made him tear it up. It had to have Chief's signature. It was such a paltry sum to our banker friend, he whipped it out of his billfold. I was astonished. Speechless. Felt foolish.

"Libbylove, remember the good advice you gave me many years ago?" He smiled sweetly, shyly. "My wife and I wanted a baby so much. We had no luck until I talked with you."

"You know I don't remember what I say!"

"This is to show our appreciation." He put the money in my hand. "Get going. Pay me when you can."

Don't tell me bankers aren't human. They have a sense of humor, too. Another banker friend made my day. Our checking account was out of balance. Out of sorts, I went to talk with him. There was no solution in sight. I confess to my banker like I do my preacher. Sometimes it is bad timing, poor arithmetic, or both. This time I was grumbling.

"You ought to give lessons."

"What are you talking about? You know all you've got to

do is empty that big pocketbook. Find those notes to yourself. You probably didn't record something."

He found it promptly. A small mistake is a mistake.

"I know bankers believe in lessons. Always going somewhere to learn something. Why don't you give lessons? Then dummies like me wouldn't pester you. You wouldn't have to put up with all this. I'd *know* how to balance my account."

"Mrs. Griffin, I don't want you to take lessons."

Dulcet tones always hook me. He had my undivided attention.

"I'd *miss* you!"

I didn't come down to earth until several days later. Chief presented me with a computer—the killjoy!

My preacher loves me best of all. It's mutual. I fill up the pew. We provide the Sunday School. When you see two carloads of scrubbed children every Sunday, it makes excuses for not attending church seem shallow. I love my doctors and teachers. I'm already in enough trouble with my dentist—he's the father of my children. My minister was there when I came. He'll be there when I leave. It's my creditors who should be my pallbearers. They have carried me this far. They should carry me all the way!

19
Friendship
(or Looking Up Old College Roommates)

"Mama, a stranger came to the door while you were gone!"

Why is it children tell some weird story when you're entertaining?

"A *stranger,* Mom!"

"You can't know everyone who comes to the door, Son. How about some coffee now, folks?"

After coffee our conversation centered around houses—the old one we were occupying and the new one we were building. The children played happily outside, except #2 child. He kept interrupting. It's not like him. I was engrossed with my guests in adult conversation, too busy commenting on the stacked building materials around Trinity Treat. Workmen were digging a ditch across the front lawn, trying to find the water line.

"While you were at the *new house,*" #1 son persisted, "that stranger came."

New house always got my attention. I listened.

"You had gone to the new house with the other children, Mama, when the stranger came." Pleased finally to have an audience, he raced on. "She was tall, beautiful, covered with furs. Her heels were on stilts. Mama," he lowered his voice, "She smelled just like a woman!"

"Tell me more."

"You should have seen her pick her way across that plank over the ditch." Delighted by his spellbound listeners, he warmed to the subject. "You should have seen that long, white Cadillac they were riding in. Took up the whole block. Had a New York license, too."

"They?"

"The lady was the only one who came to the house," he assured me. "The rest stayed in the car. They smoked cigarettes on stems out to here." He demonstrated.

"You *did* remember your manners? You *did* ask her in? You *did* tell her we were building a new home . . . and that's where I was, didn't you?"

"Oh, no, ma'am," he replied. "I just stared at her. She looked around at all the building materials. Didn't have much to say. I didn't either. She told me she was your old college roommate. She asked how many children we had. When I told her 'seven, so far,' she gasped, '*Seven!* She turned on those stilts, acting like she was in a hurry to get away!"

Silence. We were speechless. Then there was laughter unlimited. Chief sagely observed, "That'll teach her *not* to look up her old school chums!"

School chums are like that—here today, gone tomorrow. I hadn't seen that first-year college roommate in years. Friendship comes upon hard times during the years. Maturing helps, especially to realize the value of friends. Proverbs 18:24 tells us friends are few.

The Good Lord has blessed me with many friends. They are my precious jewels. Some took years to blossom. Some were instant. They have been not only enjoyable but have served as great teachers, all part and parcel of my development. The Great Teacher uses people to refine and purify me, too. He knows I make an effort to get along with everybody, even if I have to avoid them. He's watched me bypass, sidestep, go blocks—even miles—out of the way. What's worse, with no guilt. I simply rationalized: "The world is full of people I *like* to be with. Why spend my precious earthly time with those I don't enjoy?" I'm not talking about those of whom I disapprove. Just N.O.K.P.D.—"Not our kind of people, dearie!" And I'm not talking about those I *would not* be with—the ungodly. If I can't be with good people, I'd rather be alone.

But the Dear Lord won't leave me alone. He knows me. He knows I'm judgmental, intolerant, and proud. He won't let me avoid them. He plays games with me. God has a tremendous sense of humor. I love Him, but He won't leave me alone. At about the time I've thought my spiritual progress was a reality, He's brought me to a screeching halt. He not only keeps sticking that person I don't want to be with in my path, He flat out knocks me down with them!

On my knees, asking for mercy, I sense His humor. I thank Him for not giving up on me. I marvel at His methods—smart, smooth, always fascinating. I surrender. I laugh and say, "Okay. Okay, what are You trying to tell me? What is it You want me to do? Can't You call on somebody else today? Why me? You sent me Beulah not long ago. I survived. I learned to *love* her, Even like her a little. I admit it and thank You for her. One question, Lord, are You trying to teach me or both of us? Who are You working on?"

After a good laugh together, a good talk together, I thank Him for not leaving me alone—now or ever (see John 14:18). I know who needs working on—*me.* (see Mal. 3:2-3).

I realize we are commanded to "endure afflictions (see 2 Tim. 4:5). Not all afflictions are devastatingly large. Some are small, daily. Some people He places around us for our own good, to refine and purify us. He sends us help (see James 1:4) in many unexpected ways—sometimes through circumstances, sometimes through people. While I'm praying, looking, and listening, sometimes I miss it altogether. Sometimes I catch it instantly—His plan, His will for me. I never grasp the entirety of it. Not yet. Just glimpses (see 1 Cor. 13:12). Sometimes a bolt. Sometimes a dart.

He sent me one of His darts most unexpectedly one day. It was Divine—my freshman year in college. It was at a girl's school while I was walking to class. I was sort of hanging back, not wanting to be in their conversation. They were strangers to me, all except my roommate. We were becoming adjusted to each other. We had been assigned to each other. I grew up surrounded by males. It was difficult for me to like and trust other females. I didn't like what they talked about, their thought processes, their interests.

The inane chatter reached a climax. My roommate, the girl with the most flawless complexion, pushed her well-brushed eyebrows together, assumed her poor-me look, surveyed us common folk, beseeching, "Do *any* of you know what cream I should use on my face? I can't do a thing with it!"

Speechless before such beauty, drinking in her peaches-and-cream skin, everyone stopped in their tracks. They stared, stunned. Glancing around, checking the victims of this worn-out-to-me-by-now ploy, I saw envy, jealousy, admiration, even adoration. I checked my roommate. She was licking up the attention. I thought I might be sick.

"Have you ever tried *vanishing cream?*" A little voice came from the depths of the crowd. Barely audible.

The bell rang. The crowd shuffled to class. But not me, not before I saw who owned that small, soft voice, not before we shared a good laugh. She was redheaded! Frecklefaced! Put together in a unique way. She was sturdy, Not assembly-line, picture-perfect, or fragile. Her eyes were full of mirth. Her laugh was contagious. A penetrating look revealed a person filled with good will, good humor with no malice. No insult intended. A *real* beauty! I put my hand on her arm, stopping her.

"I'm not believing you! What courage!"

"Enough is enough!"

An instant friend! She was another precious jewel from Heaven. We dismissed the incident, and rarely mentioned it through the years. She didn't enjoy cutting down people. Neither did I, but I had found a kindred spirit. I had almost missed her. God had to show me.

Our friendship flowed in spite of differences. I was a night person. She, a day one. I liked people, parties, sports, and clothes. She didn't like people in bunches and never got excited about parties, ball games, or how she looked. We both liked to walk, talk, and laugh. We both had fathers who had married at age thirty. We both had been born to mothers in their forties. We were both grateful for mature parents. We both hated gossip, waste, and routine. We loved everybody, tried to like everybody. We both read our devotions each morning and said our prayers at night. We paid absolutely no attention to each other's religious bents. No comments. We were closet Christians.

Although the dear Lord sent Maisie to me and provided a good roommate for three years, our paths didn't cross for a long while. Separated by wartime, I couldn't attend her wedding. She was maid-of-honor in mine. She raised her family. I raised mine. No letters. No phone calls. Just Holy Space.

The dear Lord brought Maisie back into my life thirty years later. She had married a local boy. Nearing retirement age from the military, he and Maisie moved back to our town to be near his parents. She looked me up. Instead of a young, energetic old friend, she found an old, tired, sick one. Doctors had predicted it would be years before I'd be myself again. I had a chemical imbalance. Maisie took over where she left off. She was encouraging, supportive, and understanding (see Eccl. 4:9). She knew me (see John 15:15), and was available for badly needed counseling (see Prov. 27:9-10; Job 6:14). She remembered "the way we were." She provided needed laughs (see Prov. 17:22), was still fun, still liked to go.

When I had to go on interviews with my job, she often went along. If I wasn't functioning properly and couldn't get the right questions asked, she took over—quietly, almost unnoticed. She was sensitive to my needs. When I was discouraged, she reminded me how far I had come, pointing out progress. No longer closet Christians, we enjoyed the Lord together. We thanked Him for His dear Son together, just like we enjoyed things in the past. We both gave thanks for getting out of bed each day, keeping our children safe, even little things like finding our car keys. We thanked Him for a good friend.

Tons have been written about friendship. Signs galore decorate my house. The gracious Lord has provided me bountifully with all sizes, shapes, ages, and colors of friends. They might not win any prizes, but I'd fight you for them (see John 15:13). Kindness is the common denominator. All are interesting, fun, and good.

My newest friend, Marina, taught me to appreciate the word "good" more fully. Out of the blue one day, she asked me how I liked it.

"Hadn't thought about it. Take it for granted, I guess."

"Listen to it. Roll it around on your tongue. Think about it. 'The Lord made the world . . . and it was *good!* When you do something, say something, even cook something. Anything . . . and it's *good,* that's special. I met you. You met me. That is *good.*"

Sandy was a good BC friend—Before Children, Before World War II. Chief took another dentist's practice before going into service. He had volunteered but had not been called as yet. We moved to another new town. I enjoyed polishing my tennis, improving my new-to-me dental wife role, and learning my way into church and civic life. Children? Of course. Some day, but not now. Sandy challenged me to motherhood. She asked what-are-you-waiting-for? questions. She was a smiling, happy, Christian wife and mother—beautifully content.

I accepted the motherhood challenge. Our other friendship fruits? We brought three couples into our church. Sandy and I had found each other in church. No strangers there. Each of our mutual friends was holding out for *their* church. All were of different denominations. They couldn't agree. After a few Saturday night "see you in church's," we did. They came. One later became a leader in her area-wide church organization.

So many of my friends became leaders during my baby-birthing days. They were golf and tennis champions—a good group, especially my World War II buddies. We still have reunions and share our unique experiences sweating out the war—literally, in Alabama, where it was hot. We all praise the dear Lord for His protective arm. I learned a lot: all Texans don't brag; all only children aren't selfish; good people are everywhere—in the army and in Alabama. Being Southern isn't geographical—it's an attitude.

Mira's attitude hooked me. Back home after the war, missing my army buddies, living in the new-to-me Trinity Treat neighborhood, I spied Mira. She saw me walking my children around the block. I had seen her at PTA. She invited me into her home, and her attitude was friendly, kind, and easygoing. Her child was rolling bits of different colors of paint around in fruit jars—not watercolors but oils. The ex-art major in me jumped with joy at her allowing paint in the *house.* Unbridled creativity! Mira brought out a box of toys for my boys.

A scraggly, dirty kid appeared at the door with Mira's daughter, invited to share the fun, the food. Mira was another kindred spirit. I didn't know why the Lord sent me to her. I surely found out why he sent Mira. As usual, He didn't let me know instantly. The next morning, after I spent the night pacing the floor with a sick baby, Mira appeared from out of nowhere. She took the child from my arms and sent me to bed. She walked the baby until the doctor's office opened.

This #5 baby—#4 boy—had the dubious honor of holding the ear hospital record for having his ears opened. He had two adnoidectomys and one tonsillectomy before he was a year old. Mira was my extra pair of arms. I overheard her talking about keeping a family's children while the parents were out of town. When I asked about it, she said they were friends. She said it was a labor of love. I asked if she thought we could become friends. "Could you learn to love me that much?" She must have. I had five children when I met Mira. They babysat all nine many times. He sent me that guardian angel.

I didn't know I needed a special guardian angel. As I have mentioned earlier, I had given birth to #9 child, #8 boy and was resting in my hospital room. The morning shift of nurses was busy. My doctor had left the hospital to keep his office hours. Chief had called Tot, a dear friend who lived nearby, to come "look in on me." God Himself prompted her to run over immediately. An ex-nurse at the hospital, she visited anytime. One look at my face and she flung back the covers. I was lying in a pool of blood, in shock. She found help. Once again my Heavenly Father rescued me. He knows our every need before we do. How can we thank Him enough? Even with every breath? With praise prayers—perpetual praise prayers.

My prayers on wheels are my perpetual intercessory prayers. It is my main method of communication while driving carpools or driving, period. I ride by a sick friend's house, send up one to the dear Lord. On a long haul, I go over my prayer list. I see a soul in need along the way and send up one for him or her. I pray for the known and the unknown, friends, relatives, children, the world. I do not always pray with supplication, but for adoration too. I make confession of sins of omission and commission. And I give round-the-clock thanks, especially for my friends. I don't have much time to give, but I take time to pray. I'm involved with so many people, divided into so many pieces. I always make time for my friends. They're like family if they need me. Sometimes I pray long versions, sometimes short versions in bunches.

Bunches I love. I have my Lunch Bunch of ex-Scout-mamas. We eat once a month. Because our Scouts have flown away doesn't mean we can't keep our friendship going. My sewing group meets weekly. We not only sew but also solve problems and get out the vote. My monthly writing group encourages one another.

But my knee buddies are special. We get down on our knees and pray together. I didn't know what a treat I was missing. Now I'm an ex-closet Christian. Only after sharing a study of the Book of Acts, did I realize the exciting, satisfying life of good Christian fellowship. They're not just church-as-usual Sunday folks, but small covenant groups that are supportive, sharing, and learning to receive and release the power within us—the limitless, energizing power of the Holy Spirit and the indwelling presence of

Christ—our Savior. Jesus Christ—my very dearest Friend.

Rewards? Bill, one of God's merry men and my friend, expresses it in his own unique manner. He says, "When I cast my bread upon the waters, it comes back a ham sandwich!" (see Eccl. 11:1). Amen!

20
Mother of the Year, Father of the Year

(or Role Changing)

Every year around Mother's Day, all over the country, women are being chosen "mothers of the year."

As my kindred spirit, Erma Bombeck, has said—motherhood boasts its share of losers.

Take me for instance. I'm a natural-born loser. I get the neck of the chicken, the burnt toast. I'm only a winner at having babies. I have nothing against losers. In fact I'm always preaching to my kids to compete . . . "It's a great character-builder. You have to have losers to have winners!" And all that jazz. I believe in competition—for other people. It keeps me at that all-time low woman on the totem pole. Don't fret about it. We need cheerleaders along life's way. Losers? I know I have plenty of company.

Take this Mother-of-the-Year thing. *A contest,* they call it. It took me thirty years to make it. That's right. Our eldest had just turned thirty. A black day for me—her thirtieth. She didn't get any sympathy from me. I didn't even call her to wish her a "happy birthday!" I sent her a sympathy card and wore a black armband all day. You know I couldn't have a thirty-year-old child—not this little sweetie.

Take my husband, Chief. There's a born winner. He has me and nine healthy children. He goes to his Mama's every day for her home cooking. He has three females in his office at his beck and call and three sisters in town. That's all the other women I know about. How lucky can you get?

Chief was chosen as one of the local Fathers-of-the-Year *thirteen* years before I made it. He's a winner!

Think of all those years *I* got nine kids ready for Sunday School, found all those shoes, and shoved them out to the car. Guess who we waited for? You're right—Father-of-the-Year! He just had himself to get ready.

I'm no women's libber. I'm already liberated—a free spirit, but no libber. But with the current interest in male vs. female, I have observed inequities, especially in our local mother and father-of-the-year contests. There is a difference!

Take the announcement. Men were featured one at a time. Each day another winner was announced. It was exciting—like a continuing story, a mystery. Who's next? The women? They were announced all in one day. All their pictures and copy were crowded onto one page. The men not only had pictures but columns devoted to their child-rearing theories.

Take my article. I was introduced as "wife of the popular Dr. Griffin." He wasn't even listed as *my* husband. I was *his* wife. There were just a few sentences about me. Think of the space I could fill expounding my theories on child-rearing. I'm the one who actually did the job, the loser—me.

Chief got his due, though. Father-of-the-Year festivities weren't completely perfect, even if he strutted like a peacock, justly proud. One of the planned events was a fishing outing. He loathes fishing . . . unless he's out of town with his tombstone golfing buddies . . . without wives. Suddenly, he loves fishing.

Another event they attended en mass was a baseball game. I remember baseball. Always pregnant, I had to sit way up on a hill where the little ones could run around. I had to be ready for a quick exit to our car. Chief got to sit in the stands with the older children. It was almost worth having the baby to get to join the crew in the ballpark. Chief did enjoy the ball game with the Fathers-of-the-Year. They sat in a special box and had their names announced over the public address system, complete with introductions and applause.

They didn't take the Mothers-of-the-Year out in public. I really would have worn shoes and refrained from smoking cigars.

For their "trip," the fathers went to Washington, D.C. I laughed—to myself of course. Chief thinks Washington makes Sodom look like Reston, Va.—the planned ideal American City. He takes a dim view of my helping my favorite political candidate to get elected—afraid the nice guy will become polluted. He did manage to enjoy Washington. He said he learned something. Visions of spine-tingling sights flashed through my mind. Lincoln Memorial? White House? The Capitol? No. None of that. It was the Washington Monument. It wasn't the height that impressed Chief. It was the way one of their sponsors who accompanied them took care of the parking!

The sponsor let the honored men out at the monument. He joined them seconds later. Asked if he had any trouble parking, the sponsor merely smiled.

After a perfunctory visit, they went back to the car. It was parked right in front of the monument—*hood up!* The sponsor ushered them ceremoniously into the car like visiting dignitaries. He put the hood down and they drove off. He smilingly called out the window to honking passersby, "Car trouble, you know!"

Yes, Chief enjoyed his reign as Father-of-the-Year. He has a big, beautiful framed citation with his very own name on it. I insulted him when I suggested he hang it in the basement alongside the family pictures. No way. It's hanging in the den *over* the television!

You know television—it's the "*idiot box*" if *you're* watching it. Suddenly it becomes the "world's greatest invention" along with instant replay, if the Atlanta Falcons are playing. His citation is hung over the TV where all eyes around our house are glued. Directly underneath, on top of the TV, are his golf and tennis trophies. He's proud of them all—especially the one for Father-of-the-Year. My mild protest that, "You didn't do a thing your friends or neighbors wouldn't be glad to do for you," went unheard and ignored. Like the trophy I added to his collection that read, "The World's Greatest Lover." Many a wife thinks her husband is the world's greatest lover. But she can never catch him at it. That's not true in our household. He catches me!

The children, bless them, were really concerned about my morale. They asked, "Where are *your awards,* Libbylove?"

"What awards?" I whimpered. "I haven't won an award since the Orange County Declamation Contest in the second grade!"

They looked around for something. One spied a trophy.

"Here's one Chief's golfing buddy gave you, 'The World's Most Patient Wife!' "

I joined their game. I found an ashtray a friend gave me on a birthday that said, "It's not the end of the world. It's the end of an era!" I fitted it with hooks and we all searched for a place to hang it. They found a tiny wall—all the room I needed—in our bedroom. I glued together an old broken fraternity plaque Chief gave me before we married. There were three Greek letters on the front. On its backside were scrawled their meaning, "First. Last. Always." In his own handwriting. Next to it, they hung a framed, hand-painted wedding invitation—ours. Our wedding picture hung alongside. In it, I'm drooling over him. Chief? He's grinning, looking straight ahead at the photographer. Those were for starters—important things. They were hung handily on the wall next to Chief's sock drawer. He couldn't miss them.

The reason it took me thirty years, thirteen years after Chief to make it as one of the local Mothers-of-the-Year, is that I'm a slow learner. Had to learn to listen to the children, get on their training program. The kids are smarter than we were. Ask them.

"Libbylove, you've got to do your own thing."

"What's that?"

"You do what *you* want to do. Everybody today does their own thing. What do you want to do?"

That stumped me. Been so long since I had done what I wanted to do, I couldn't remember what it was. I gave it some thought. I decided I wanted to write.

All went well. I slipped out to writing classes on Monday nights. No one missed me. All were fed, sleepy, or doing last-minute homework. Chief sacked out after a strenuous weekend of golf and tennis. Everything was great. I was happy as a bug until I blew it. I was in a hurry, had to do my homework.

My assignment was to write a confession story. You can't write confession stories unless you read confession stories. I was struggling to bring the groceries in one day. Out slipped one of those magazines—lurid headlines with pictures to match. Sprawled over the front porch. The kids were trying to catch the stuff flying out of the grocery bag. I tried to catch those magazines. No way. The magazines were snatched up first. Then they rested upon the culprit—red-faced me!

My explanations went unheeded as they chorused, "You'll *never* make Mother-of-the-Year." It was the first time but not the last. It became a cry they used after that to keep me in line.

It looked like a foregone conclusion that I'd never make Mother-of-the-Year. Chief even offered to take me to Williamsburg, Virginia—the "trip" for the honored moms. You don't know what a concession that was—the here-and-now man taking me to an historic place!

I longed to see Williamsburg. I am a lover of old things, old friends, old cars, old shoes, old furniture, and old girdles. I knew better than to ask. I remembered Mount Vernon. Couldn't erase that jaunt from my mind. Chief stopped the car outside the gates. He gave me fifteen minutes. One of the children had lost Chief's shirt in the car. The world's greatest lover wouldn't tour Mount Vernon without a coat and tie.

Glad I couldn't see myself—pregnant, rushing around that gorgeous place with five kids in tow. The guides were stunned when I said, "No, thank you. We can't join the guided tour. I just have *fifteen minutes.*" They didn't know whether to call an ambulance or the police. They stared. I advised them to "Carry on. Ignore me." They took my advice.

I couldn't chance Williamsburg. It looked like more than a fifteen-minute job. Chief insisted on taking me *by* Williamsburg once, riding down the highway anyway. We'd been to a member-guest golfing weekend in New York. He knew he was safe. I was about to become a first-time grandmother.

I couldn't waste time getting home. My grandchild was overdue. You know she couldn't have had that baby without me, not my daughter. I wasn't about to do anything as foolish as Williamsburg. If you think mothering's important, just think about grandmothering. They don't call it "grand" for nothing. I blew it again—no Williamsburg. There went my chance.

Visions of the historic place flew through my mind when I received the phone call.

"You have been selected as one of the five Mothers-of-the-Year."

"Not me. I couldn't accept it. Every year someone gets this notion because I have so many children. They ought to wait until I get them over Fool's Hill. I used to be able to get the word to the selection committee, "Not me! Where did I foul up?"

"We don't select them that way anymore. It's a letter-writing campaign now."

"Don't pay any attention to letters. Not fair! I have more children to write."

"Not just your children or your friends. Your daughters-in-law, too!" (Silence) "You *can't* disappoint all those people who love you, who went to all that trouble!" (Silence) "I'm not hanging up until you say, 'yes.' Don't be ridiculous."

Not one to go around disappointing people, I succumbed.

My loser streak showed up anyway. They were not going to take the moms to Williamsburg, due to a gas shortage. It was to be New Bern, North Carolina. (We really *should* see our own state first.)

I didn't care about being Mother-of-the-Year. I wanted a leisurely trip to Williamsburg to drink in every brick. What a shock!

It wasn't the last one. Take the citation bit. I was consoling myself. I'd have something to hang on that wall the kids rigged up for "my awards." Another first. They gave me a citation that proclaimed me an honorary citizen of the town. There was no mention of Mother-of-the-Year. The town I live in now is an arch-rival, sportswise, to the neighboring town I was born and raised in. I would have been an honorary citizen of the enemy's town!

I was determined to enjoy the honor even if I didn't have time or inclination. At least the kids would quit trying to keep me in line, particularly the three in college. You know college nowadays—"A fountain of knowledge where they all go to drink." The first event for the Mother-of-the-Year was coffee at 8:30 AM, before the shopping mall opened. (Merchants of our town sponsor the contest.) I hadn't been anywhere at 8:30 in years except to schools. I thought I shouldn't clog the streets and make working people late. I never did.

We could invite six people. I couldn't think of six people I wanted to make miserable at that time of the morning. After much thought, I sent invitations to those I suspected of bestowing this honor upon me.

The next event was a downtown hotel luncheon. I was fifteen minutes late. By the time my children related the story, it became an hour—like the game of gossip. I was unavoidably late, due to a doctor's appointment. I wouldn't tell him about my "honor." So what? But I was mortified. I was holding up the works and worse, the photographer, the flower-pinner-oners, and the food. In spite of everything the floor refused to swallow me up. In this pinch, I said the only thing I knew how—honest. It hurts. I proclaimed to all, "I told you I didn't have time to be Mother-of-the-Year!" as I made my way to the head table.

Finally I got my nerve up to look around. Who in the world would give up precious time for such? Familiar faces loomed in view—townswomen I knew, friends, acquaintances, past Mothers-of-the-Year. They were all sweet, understanding, and marvelous. I was proud to become a member of this group—groupie that I am. I was most humble, (see Ps. 113:9; Eph. 6:2) and honored.

The restoration of Tryon Palace that I saw in New Bern was most impressive. Forget Williamsburg. It's probably too commercial anyway. It was worth it all to see my children happy for me. They come in from school singing, "Here come the Children-of-the-Year!" Then they came by my typewriter, gave me a kiss, and moved on, declaring me, "Nut of the Year!"

As usual, they are so right.

Don't despair. You, too, might be Mother-of-the-Year someday—a winner. Everyone loves a winner. Listen to your husband and children. Unless you are a born loser, like myself, it might be sooner than you think! Lots of luck!

21
The Totaled Woman
(or Reaping the Results of Beauty and Charm School)

When I signed up for "The Total Woman" course, everybody laughed. Especially Chief. Aren't you in enough trouble? Do you really want to be any more attractive? Why? Are you getting in shape for another husband?

Chief wasn't the only one who questioned me. After my dental-wives buddies quit laughing, they asked the same question—Why? They should know I'm a perennial student who takes every course I can manage. I could manage this. It was available for dental wives attending the annual state meeting.

Recently I learned about the tucks you can take in your body, from top to toe, and in between. I had been saving for it, my tucks and my money. So now I was ready. They didn't think I was going to miss the "Total Woman," did they? All that fun? No way. I wanted to be where the action was. Marabel Morgan was and is my kind of woman. She makes things happen. She's full of surprises, all good. She's a person you can turn inside out, and she's still beautiful. Whatever it is she's got, it comes in the room with her. I need that.

I need beauty. I've talked with the dear Lord about this, and blamed Him. He made me this way—gave me a mom who looked for and found beauty in all things. I look for it. I find it—in a responsive laugh, in an understanding look, in a wink, a hug, a Carolina cardinal preening, in an unexpected gardenia bloom, and in bouncing babies.

I have a thing about babies—cherubs. I love them. I share Mother Teresa's thoughts: "Every child is like a baby Jesus. Every abortion a crucifixion. God will provide, even if at the last moment or in unexpected ways".

I love cherubs. I can't wait to see God's collection—all those cherubs and angels singing and playing, around His throne, having a time.

I know God has a sense of humor. He must enjoy a good joke because He made so many of us! There's so much false reverence, so much solemnity, so many claims of "my way." Not His way. No wonder so many people aren't sure they want to go to heaven. They're afraid it will be no fun, full of phonies. That's strange jargon. My mom always said to stop, look, and listen. You might hear a lot of mumbo jumbo. If there are no smiles, no laughs, no joy, then you're in the wrong place. Christians should be the happiest people in the world. They have more reason to be. They have hope. They know about heaven.

Maisie told me I'd never make the heavenly choir. Singing? Forget it. There's no call for croakers. Sure I can work on rainbows? How I love color! Maisie doubts it. She said I'd never keep the lines straight. She knows me. Nothing can keep me away from hanging around the sunsets. Except the Heavenly Chief. My mom made me promise I'd think of her whenever they appeared. I keep my promises. She'd be painting those rainbows. She'd let me help. Moms are like that.

My mom's partially to blame for my love of beauty. She insisted that I look my best. I owe it to others. Then forget self. I try. Still fidget with scarves though I have no neck. I change heel heights for a well-proportioned total look, just as she taught me.

It's not my mom's fault I'm not a "Total Woman." She tried. She gave me lessons galore in how to walk, how to talk, and how to act. During my college-town childhood, neighborhood children were recruited often as human guinea pigs. Lessons were free. I was part of educational experiments conducted by and for teachers.

One of my teachers married a "Total Woman." Kay Kyser, the famous band leader, taught me to do the charleston. He boarded at our hotel during his college days. He later married Georgia Carroll, the singer with his band. She was the total woman of my era—my ideal, a model and singer. I kept scrapbooks of her pictures, her beauty secrets. It's no secret, she's a "Total Woman."

It's not easy to be a "Total Woman": a good housekeeper, loving homemaker, and super love partner. My losing streak always appears. I flunk housekeeping hands down. As a loving homemaker, I'm a natural. Super love partner? Wouldn't want to be any better. What you sow, you reap (see Gal. 6:7).

Some of my children call before they come. Considerate? Questionable. Meanest Mom might have been at the typewriter all day, not at the sink. I'm not known for my clean closets or lovely lawn. Loving homemaker? Yes. Bedlam's still open to all (see Rom. 12:13; 1 Tim. 5:10)—those who like to take chances, like surprises.

Super love partner? Me? You can't beat results. God made women responders. Don't blame Him for frigid women or lousy lovers. Impatient teachers or underachievers. Goethe said it: "Women are to be loved, not understood."

Priority setting is an important part of being a complete person. It advocates putting your husband and children's needs before church, civic, and social. Who takes care of the total woman's needs? Our Heavenly Father! It's too big a load to put on a husband, friend, or lover.

I was guilty—guilty of unknowingly putting the yoke of my needs on Chief. Not only my financial needs, but emotional, physical, mental, and spiritual. I was guilty of allowing Chief's moods to govern my day (see Prov. 16:5-6). To make it or break it. It's okay to be a responder in bed. Out of bed, it's a different matter (see Prov. 15:13). I tried to make our home a haven—fun, nice to come home to. I agree with Proverbs 15:15" . . . but he that is of a merry heart hath a continual feast."

I not only enjoyed merry hearts, I openly admired beautiful people. Beauty was not at the top of my totem pole of self-seeking, but a notch on it. I secretly disliked fat people. I never admitted to myself. I filed it under failure to control one's appetite, failure to care about self or others. I was intolerant, judgmental (see Matt. 7:1). I didn't have the problem then—certainly not as a "premy," a child, teener, or young lady. Even after nine children, I had only twenty accumulative pounds to shed. I lost it, then gained it back. No starches, sweets or fruits were allowed. The second time around my body totally rejected the prescribed diet, resulting in flip-flop blood sugar, hourly mood swings, and slowed mental and physical processes—a chemical imbalance.

Instead of losing twenty pounds, I gained forty. In three months! While on a diet! It was scary. Ensuing dejection, confusion, and depression resulted. I was incapable of helping myself—a first for me. Usually, if I tried harder, I'd get the desired results. Not this time. There was no progress for a year.

The only thing that kept me going was my deep faith. I just couldn't believe He barely let me into this world, rewarded me with nine blessings, and then would abandon me. Not my Heavenly Father—the Comforter and Protector. He sent rescuers—guardian angels. Through Chief, He got me to the right place, none too early by my timetable. I was on my knees—prostrate—the Totaled Woman.

The medical help The Great Physician sent me cautioned me to expect no overnight recovery. At my age, it's a slow process. I thank God for it. It gave me ample time to contemplate, meditate, and confess. I view fat, infirm, incomplete children of God in a totally different light. We all are handicapped—one way or another.

I thank God I'm a *Totaled Woman.* He didn't total me. (see James 1:13). I needed it (see Mal. 3:3). Our Father doesn't total us. He uses troubles, tests, and trials to refine us. The dear Lord isn't through with me yet. It takes time. It took me awhile to become the fat, free, unblenching butterfly that I am. I'm still enjoying His gift (see James 1:4).

Epilogue

When you like surprises, and are blessed with nine children, you are going to have surprises.

I was surprised by more pleasures, by far, than pains. I found a built-in audience for my day-to-day productions. They laughed at my lyrics, sung off-key to "Reuben, Reuben, I've been thinking." They never denounced or derided my dancing feet, never complained about my creative cooking. They suffered through my sewing sessions, my Mickey Mouse theories, my Libbynese, and my lipsticked kisses.

They did far more for me than I did for them. They developed my latent talents, fulfilled my suppressed desires, developed my patience, my staying power, my organizational and managerial abilities. They fulfilled my acting desires—acting interested when busy, alive when half-dead, calm when worried. I'm like the duck, smooth on top, paddling like fury underneath.

My children gave me lots of love and laughter, provided opportunities to practice salesmanship, persuasiveness, and charm. They enabled me to go-go-go to my heart's content, to mingle with the masses, to appreciate peace and quiet. They stretched my brain, my back, imagination, and pocketbook.

I thank them for making me a mother who could sleep.

They made me mad. They made me glad, but they never betrayed my trust. I thank them for brightening, enriching, and understanding our marriage by watching, helping, and encouraging Chief and me grow up. With love.

Children are the sunshine of life—full of trust, zest, and surprises. They are my blessings. I thank God for them, especially for giving me more reasons to call on Him, for catapulting me closer to my Comforter, Confidant, Constant Companion, and Creator from Whom all blessings flow.

I still like surprises. I learned the greatest surprises happen when I leave it to the Lord. He makes things happen. Life with Him is a party, an adventure full of surprises. I am wild about Abundant Life—asking and receiving, asking and receiving. My cup runneth over!